FIFTY YEARS WITH FATHER HESBURGH

FIFTY YEARS WITH

Father Hesburgh

ON AND OFF THE RECORD

ROBERT SCHMUHL

University of Notre Dame Press
Notre Dame, Indiana

University of Notre Dame Press
Notre Dame, Indiana 46556
www.undpress.nd.edu

Manufactured in the United States of America

Library of Congress Cataloging-in-Publication Data

Names: Schmuhl, Robert, author.
Title: Fifty years with Father Hesburgh : on and off the record / Robert
 Schmuhl.
Description: Notre Dame, Indiana : University of Notre Dame Press, 2016.
Identifiers: LCCN 2016019556 (print) | LCCN 2016030895 (ebook) | ISBN
 9780268100896 (hardcover : alk. paper) | ISBN 9780268100919 (pdf) | ISBN
 9780268100926 (epub)
Subjects: LCSH: Hesburgh, Theodore M. (Theodore Martin), 1917-2015. |
 University of Notre Dame--Presidents--Biography. | University of Notre
 Dame--History--20th century.
Classification: LCC LD4112.1 .S35 2016 (print) | LCC LD4112.1 (ebook) |
 DDC 378.772/89—dc23
LC record available at https://lccn.loc.gov/2016019556

∞ *This paper meets the requirements of ANSI/NISO Z39.48-1992*
(Permanence of Paper).

For alumni, students, faculty, and others

who are beneficiaries of Father Hesburgh's

transformation of Notre Dame

and his affirmation of

"the humane imperative"

Contents

Acknowledgments

Sections of some chapters that follow appeared earlier, either in my book, *The University of Notre Dame: A Contemporary Portrait* (University of Notre Dame Press, 1986) or in articles I wrote over the years for *Notre Dame Magazine*. Previously published material has been revised or adapted to focus more directly on Rev. Theodore M. Hesburgh, C.S.C. I'm grateful to Notre Dame Press and to the editors of *Notre Dame Magazine* for their permission to extract passages from what I had already written, especially many quotations from extended interviews I conducted with Father Hesburgh, beginning in the 1980s.

The chapter about the U.S. presidents that Father Hesburgh knew and, in most cases, worked with exists solely because of the foresight of Robert Costa. A former prized student and now a prizewinning national political reporter for *The Washington Post*, Bob and his crew videotaped the conversation with Father Hesburgh for NDtv. This conversation took place during a regular session of my spring 2008 American Studies course, American Political Life.

Two administrative assistants at Notre Dame—Katie Schlotfeldt in the Department of American Studies and Mary Jo Young in the John W. Gallivan Program in Journalism,

Ethics and Democracy—helped in many ways to prepare the manuscript. Katie transcribed two of the extended interviews, while Jo printed and organized different drafts of each chapter.

Several people provided information or pictures for this book, including Melanie Chapleau, Matt Cashore, Carolyn Hardman, Mandy Kinnucan, Charles Lamb, Joe Raymond, Matt Storin, Kerry Temple, Amanda Retartha, Thomas Tweed, and Kevin Whelan.

Michael Schmuhl, Notre Dame class of 2005 and a third-generation Domer in our family, read the (semi)final text closely and made numerous suggestions that I incorporated into the version delivered to the publisher.

At the Notre Dame Press, I owe a special debt of gratitude to Stephen M. Wrinn, the director, and Stephen Little, the acquisitions editor. As copy editor, Kellie M. Hultgren improved the text by pointing out and correcting certain infelicities.

Once again, Judy Schmuhl proved to be the perfect wife for an obsessed writer, letting me keep my home office door shut (with a Do Not Disturb sign posted) while this book came into being. She even had to amuse herself on some mornings during our trip to Europe in the summer of 2015, when I needed time to draft one of the chapters.

Rev. Theodore M. Hesburgh, C.S.C., Through the Years

1917   Born on May 25 in Syracuse, New York

1934   Enrolled at the University of Notre Dame and en-
        tered the Congregation of Holy Cross

1939   Earned a bachelor of philosophy degree from the
        Gregorian University in Rome

1943   Ordained a Holy Cross priest at Sacred Heart Church
        (now Basilica) at Notre Dame

1945   Received doctorate in theology from Catholic Uni-
        versity of America (Washington, DC) and returned
        to Notre Dame to teach religion and to serve as chap-
        lain for World War II veterans on campus

1948   Named chairman of Notre Dame's Department of
        Religion

1949   Selected to be executive vice president of Notre Dame,
        a post he held until 1952

1952   Appointed the fifteenth president of Notre Dame at
        age thirty-five, beginning thirty-five years in that
        office

1954   Received appointment from President Dwight D. Eisenhower to the National Science Board, the first of sixteen presidential appointments, a seat he held until 1966

1956   Named permanent Vatican representative to the International Atomic Energy Agency in Vienna, a position lasting until 1970

1957   Appointed by President Eisenhower to be a charter member of the U.S. Commission on Civil Rights; subsequently named chairman of the commission by President Richard Nixon in 1969 but forced to step down by the White House in 1972 for exposing hiring practices in the federal government at variance with civil rights law

1961   Named to the Board of Trustees of the Rockefeller Foundation; chair of the trustees from 1977 to 1982

1962   Profiled in a *Time* magazine cover article about Catholic intellectuals

1963   Served as chairman of the International Federation of Catholic Universities, a post he held until 1970

1964   Awarded the Medal of Freedom by President Lyndon B. Johnson in a White House ceremony, the youngest of thirty recipients including Aaron Copland, Walt Disney, T. S. Eliot, Helen Keller, Walter Lippmann, Reinhold Niebuhr, and John Steinbeck

1967   Shepherded the transfer of Notre Dame governance from the Congregation of Holy Cross to a board of trustees composed of both religious and lay members

1968   Named by Pope Paul VI to head the Vatican's delegation to the conference celebrating the twentieth anniversary of the United Nations' Universal Declaration of Human Rights

1969   Wrote a nationally discussed letter to the Notre Dame community about the limits of protest on campus that became known as the fifteen-minute rule, stating that a quarter hour of meditation would be allowed before the university took action against demonstrators

1970   After the National Guard's shooting of protesters at Kent State, announced in a petition called the Hesburgh Declaration that the United States should end involvement in the Vietnam War

1971   Served as chairman of the Overseas Development Council, a position he held until 1982

1972   Championed the admission of women to Notre Dame, ending the all-male undergraduate student body that had existed for 130 years

1972   Built, at the request of Pope Paul VI, the Ecumenical Institute in Tantur, Jerusalem, to promote greater religious understanding and collaborative undertakings

1974   Appointed by Pope Paul VI to be a member of the Holy See's delegation to the United Nations

1974   Published *The Humane Imperative: A Challenge for the Year 2000* (Yale University Press)

1974   Named by President Gerald Ford to the Presidential Clemency Board, his sixth White House appointment

1979   Nominated by President Jimmy Carter to be the first Catholic priest to serve as a U.S. ambassador to lead the American delegation to the U.N. Conference on Science and Technology for Development

1979   Appointed by President Carter to serve as chairman of the Select Commission on Immigration and Refugee Policy, which conducted its work for three years

1979   Published *The Hesburgh Papers: Higher Values in Higher Education* (Andrews and McMeel)

1983   Named by Pope John Paul II to the Pontifical Council for Culture

1984   Awarded an honorary degree—his one hundredth—from Notre Dame

1987   Retired as president of Notre Dame on June 1, shortly after celebrating his seventieth birthday

1989   Named founding cochair of the reform-proposing Knight Commission on Intercollegiate Athletics, work that continued until 2001

1990   Named to Harvard University's Board of Overseers and in 1994 elected president of the board, serving two years in that role

1990   Published his autobiography, *God, Country, Notre Dame* (Doubleday), which became a national best seller

1991   Appointed by President George H. W. Bush to the board of directors of the United States Institute of Peace, service that continued to 2000

1992   Published *Travels with Ted and Ned* (Doubleday)

1999   Completed fact-finding trip to refugee camps in Kosovo for the United Nations

2000   Awarded the Congressional Gold Medal in the U.S. Capitol, the first figure in higher education so honored

2002   Appointed by President George W. Bush to the Commission on Presidential Scholars, his sixteenth presidential appointment

2002   Received his 150th honorary degree (the most awarded to any person), from the University of San Diego

2004   Became the inaugural recipient of the National Collegiate Athletic Association's Gerald R. Ford Award for leadership in intercollegiate athletics

2013 Visited Washington, DC, for the last time on May 22, a trip that included a twenty-minute White House meeting with President Barack Obama and a congressional celebration of his ninety-sixth birthday in the U.S. Capitol

2015 Passed away the evening of February 26 at Holy Cross House on the Notre Dame campus after celebrating Mass that morning

In the fall of 1964, William E. Miller and his wife, Stephanie, attended a Notre Dame home football game with Father Hesburgh. A 1935 Notre Dame alumnus and a member of the U.S. House of Representatives, Miller was running for vice president as Senator Barry Goldwater's Republican running mate at the time. Photo courtesy of the *South Bend Tribune*.

Prologue

"You're always welcome here."

Father Hesburgh had finished telling the last of his stories during our conversation and extended his hand to say goodbye. A student was waiting outside his office to read that day's *New York Times* to him.

Visibly more frail than in our previous visit a few weeks earlier, he had talked almost exclusively about the distant past during this discussion. A question about Frank Leahy triggered a memory of traveling to the distraught football coach's home after a defeat by Michigan State and trying to bring him out of his self-imposed funk. With a winning percentage of .855 and six (of eleven) undefeated seasons, losing at any time was alien to every gene in Leahy's body. However, Father Hesburgh, new to the university presidency and a decade younger than the famous coach, decided personal intervention was required. So he took both executive and priestly action.

With attention to precise details, he talked with me in his clear, direct, often wry way. Our meeting took place late in 2014. It began with him mentioning the possibility of reaching a hundred years old. (He was then approaching ninety-eight.) I responded that I had figured out he would be around for his 105th birthday, and he wondered why I said that.

"That way your life would have the perfect symmetry of three thirty-five-year periods," I answered, and then sketched out what I meant. The first thirty-five included his youth, education, ordination, and first years at Notre Dame (teaching religion and serving as chaplain for World War II veterans, and becoming executive vice president at age thirty-two). The second encompassed his presidency of the university as well as numerous Washington, New York, and Vatican appointments. The third featured his retirement years of continued involvement in projects both inside and outside Notre Dame and the attainment of near-universal status, on campus at least, as "everybody's grandfather."

Regrettably, both Father Hesburgh and I overshot the mark. Late in the evening of February 26, 2015, he passed away. He had offered Mass that morning and prayed the rosary (in French) not long before taking his last breath.

For a half century Father Hesburgh had fascinated me. Even before I became a Notre Dame student in 1966, I had begun to follow what he said and to seek out what he did. During the tumultuous late 1960s I covered him and Notre Dame for the Associated Press and other journalistic outlets. For a young reporter, occupying a front-row seat during that time provided a valuable education in itself. Father Hesburgh was in his prime as an educational leader in America and a public figure with international stature. In the nomenclature of news, he was good copy. In my juvenile journalistic assessment, he was very good copy and genuinely interesting to boot.

After graduate school and a post-Watergate sojourn in politics, I returned to Notre Dame in 1980 and, before long, started to ask Father Hesburgh to speak at campus events. He never declined. A few years later I began interviewing him for book and magazine projects. As far as I was concerned, he remained good—indeed, engrossing—copy, and these sessions often took turns into subjects he wanted to discuss outside the scope of whatever I was asking him about and, at a particular moment, writing.

Those turns, over time, evolved into friendship. I still imposed on him to say grace at special dinners—the last being in 2011—but I also made a point of stopping by his office, 1315, high atop the Theodore M. Hesburgh Library, or his apartment in Holy Cross House next to Moreau Seminary on the Notre Dame campus.

No topic was off-limits. After an exchange of pleasantries and an inquiry about his health—to which he invariably responded, "Not bad for an old goat"—Father frequently asked, "What should I know?"

Did he want to talk about someone or something at Notre Dame? Were recent actions of the current U.S. president on his mind? Was the threat of terrorism that day's concern? Truth be told, Father more often than not breezed by his own question with some alacrity and began to explain what was on *his* mind that day. I listened and chimed in with a remark or a request for him to comment on a subject in more detail. Words always came easily to him. Some stories even seemed on a continuous loop in his repertoire of remembering. What was remarkable, however, was that the second, third, or tenth retelling followed the same exact lines. He knew the script of his past, word for word.

During most of our conversations he'd recount a new story, like the one about Frank Leahy. In the last decade of his life he worried aloud about, as he bluntly said, "losing my marbles"—colloquial phrases always came naturally, creating instant rapport with listeners—but he never lost command of memorable events in his own memorable life.

Father Hesburgh spoke at length about his history—his story—because he knew my work of writing about American presidents and Notre Dame history often intersected with his personal experience. As an unreformed newshound, I kept asking questions, probing more deeply for details and context. Through his memory he could relive moments high and low, public and private, sacred and profane. His eager listener was something of a link to his past and a sometime source of contemporary gossip. You might say our visits were mutually rewarding. I loved hearing his stories, and he seemed to enjoy keeping up with matters, near and far, from a congenital reporter and (sorry to say) connoisseur of rumor.

From time to time after 2000, Father Hesburgh raised the possibility of collaborating on a book. "You're the writer," he'd say. One time he even proposed bringing a tape recorder to our conversations, a clear hint of his interest in preserving what we discussed. Unfortunately, other writing projects and assignments to teach abroad kept me away for semester-long stretches, and he dropped the idea. But, being that congenital reporter, I jotted down notes about many of our conversations. I also made sure to save the letters he sent—each one of his is signed "Father Ted," yet mine to him keep the more formal salutation of "Dear Father Hesburgh"—and I also squirrelled away articles he wrote and interviews he gave. These sources often formed the bases for our interviews or conversations. I followed up on what he said to learn more.

Starting in 1985, I conducted a series of extended, on-the-record interviews with Father Hesburgh about his service as Notre Dame president and other duties from 1952 until right before his retirement in 1987; his recollections of the turmoil on campus and elsewhere during the 1960s; his memories of the U.S. presidents he knew and worked with; and his assessment of the years after he left the university's presidency but tried to remain as active as he could. These interviews—Father Hesburgh in his own words—provide the spine (and brain) of most of the following chapters.

As you'd expect, some passages from the interviews were trimmed for the sake of relevance and continuity. Even for a figure of well-known eloquence, a spoken sentence can include an occasional extraneous or misplaced word. Light editing here and there makes a statement more readable in its published form. Of course, there are no alterations to Father Hesburgh's meaning or the thrust of his arguments. On occasion you will find the repetition of a particular point or experience, often in his words. If it was integral to what he was explaining, there seemed to me no reason to remove it, and additional context has virtue within a chapter.

Judy Schmuhl, devoted wife and helpmate for more years than a first-grader can count, chides me for being a "methodical packrat," a compulsive saver of items, many now approaching antique status. Indeed, in our basement I have several folders of articles about Father Hesburgh composed by a young reporter during the late 1960s and the spring of 1970. The first chapter draws from these yellowing dispatches, especially quotations I collected at campus news conferences that the then president conducted.

As this book began to take shape, I considered adding the phrase "A Memoir" as a subtitle. That, however, would have been an inaccurate description of my intention. The word *memoir* puts the focus on the author. This book is about Father Hesburgh, with the narrator providing some explanatory, though admittedly personal, context along the way. You might call the genre here "biographical memoir." Father Hesburgh's life and recollections are the raisons d'être for each section. It is *his* book, with the author something of an amanuensis.

Though this work is biographical, it's important to underline at the outset that what follows is not a full-fledged, cradle-to-coffin biography. Someone else will take responsibility for the multiple-year project of studying Father Hesburgh's official and private papers from his years as Notre Dame president, U.S. government and Vatican appointee, board member, engaged world citizen, and all the rest. It will be a Herculean task to relate the entirety of this crowded and eventful life. For my part, all of the notes, files, letters, and tapes related to this book will be given to the Notre Dame Archives, making my wife quite happy.

Almost every time we talked Father Hesburgh puffed on a cigar, and he was unfailingly generous in having a friend join him. Charitable alumni and friends enabled his habit, even after the university announced it would be forevermore a smoke-free environment. For Father Hesburgh, that edict went too far. This singular pleasure trumped institutional—rather than clerical—obedience. While he declared (in a widely quoted remark) that voting should be considered "a civic sacrament," cigars produced for him (I imagined) secular incense instead of secondhand smoke.

Father Hesburgh hated discrimination of all kinds, including—in his judgment—"prejudice against cigar smokers." In his post-presidency journal, *Travels with Ted & Ned* (1992), he relates an anecdote that shows how personally he took the efforts to extinguish his enjoyment while cruising in the Caribbean on the *Queen Elizabeth II* in 1988: "We had to change our usual place in the Princess Grill tonight because someone objected to our cigars. We were moved into an area at the other side of the room where everybody else smoked cigars and welcomed us. Our friends at the old location said they were going to put on a revolution and all start smoking cigars because they didn't want us to leave. Some of them came over to have their pictures taken with us. But there is always someone who objects loudly, thinking that cigar smokers are just a notch above mass murderers."

One time when we were conversing, he spoke of "a spot" on his lung, but that wasn't enough to cause him much worry or the abandonment of a routine (ritual, really) he relished. Before his funeral, a somewhat rebellious yet always caring *confrère* in the Holy Cross order surreptitiously tucked a fresh

Cuban cigar up the cuff of Father Hesburgh's shirt. He went to his eternal reward with a stogie, celestial or otherwise, near at hand.

Lewis Mumford, one of America's most respected and perceptive literary figures of the twentieth century, titled his autobiography *Sketches from Life*. Many vignettes in this volume could be classified instead as "sketches from memory." What Father Hesburgh did and said remains so vivid in my mind that the words and actions could have happened yesterday.

I can even date the first time I watched Father Hesburgh intently and came away impressed with him both as a speaker and as a priest. It was October 3, 1964, and William E. Miller, Barry Goldwater's running mate, had come back to his alma mater to campaign for the Republican ticket and to attend a football game against Purdue. A longtime member of the House of Representatives from upstate New York, Miller delivered his stump speech from the porch of Sorin Hall.

A high-school student at the time and already fascinated with politics, I attended this rally out of personal interest and familial fealty. My father, a Notre Dame alumnus of the class of 1936, knew Miller, class of 1935, from their student days. Though the elder in our household never comprehended why anyone would want to follow American political life as devotedly as he kept up with Notre Dame football and basketball— he had season tickets in both sports for many decades—this was the second time during the fall of 1964 that we had gone to hear Miller speak. At the first event, near our home, I had even met the candidate.

On that long-ago October day at Notre Dame, without suggesting a personal endorsement or institutional support, Father Hesburgh told the crowd, estimated in news reports at 2,500, that the university was proud to have a graduate running for national office for the first time in history. After a speech asking students to become involved in democratic activities—the candidate's refrain "whether you do anything about it or whether you don't" still echoes in my head—Miller and Father Hesburgh left their places at Sorin Hall to head to the South Bend Airport. I'm not sure why, but we decided to follow the motorcade in our own car.

We arrived at the airport to see Miller go up the steps of his plane. As it moved to the runway for takeoff, I became more interested in watching Father Hesburgh, who remained standing outside his car, than the maneuvering of the aircraft. Without looking around for witnesses, Father Hesburgh raised his right arm and offered a blessing for the travelers, complete with a large Sign of the Cross. It was moving and memorable, then and today.

To check the exact date of the Purdue game in 1964, I looked up the campus newspaper of that era, *The Voice*, a weekly precursor to *The Observer*, which started weekday publication in 1966. Miller's talk headlines page one, but other articles on that page announce upcoming visits of Hubert H. Humphrey, the Democratic vice-presidential nominee; R. Sargent Shriver, director of the Peace Corps and the war on poverty; and Supreme Court Justice Arthur J. Goldberg. All in a week's time. Notre Dame was becoming a regular stop for Washington's leaders, and Father Hesburgh's work there (in 1964 he was serving on the National Science Board and the U.S. Commission on Civil Rights) was no doubt partially responsible. In Humphrey's remarks, quoted the following week in *The Voice*, he called Father Hesburgh "one of the truly outstanding men of our time."

That statement wasn't political hyperbole. A few weeks earlier, on September 14, President Lyndon Johnson had given Father Hesburgh the Medal of Freedom, the nation's highest civilian honor, saying, "Educator and humanitarian, he has inspired a generation of students and given of his wisdom in the struggle for the rights of man." The priest was the youngest Medal of Freedom recipient that day in the White House ceremony. Some of the others included (in alphabetical order) Aaron Copland, Walt Disney, T. S. Eliot, Helen Keller, Walter Lippmann, Lewis Mumford, Reinhold Niebuhr, Carl Sandburg, and John Steinbeck. Impressive company, to say the least.

Earlier that year, on June 21, 1964, Father Hesburgh joined hands with Rev. Martin Luther King Jr. in singing "We Shall Overcome" at a rally in Chicago's Soldier Field. Less than two weeks after that event, captured in a memorable picture of these two religious and civil rights leaders that now hangs in the National Portrait Gallery in Washington, President Johnson signed into law the Civil Rights Act of 1964, which Father Hesburgh was instrumental in formulating.

Two years after the eventful fall of 1964—Johnson and Humphrey were decisive victors over Goldwater and Miller, 61.1 percent to 38.5 percent, in the November election—I became a Notre Dame student. Opportunities to see Father Hesburgh occurred more often—especially as reporting assignments involving him came up—but even those sightings proved sporadic. A popular campus joke circulated then:

"What's the difference between God and Father Hesburgh?"

"God is everywhere. Father Hesburgh is everywhere except Notre Dame."

Decades later, when travel became next to impossible for him, Father Hesburgh offered the hint of a smile when someone repeated the good-natured jest.

This portrait of Father Hesburgh appeared frequently in the press during what he called "the student revolution" and as part of the widespread coverage about his "fifteen-minute rule" of 1969 to deal with student protests. Photo courtesy of the University of Notre Dame Archives.

ONE

Ted the Head

Father Hesburgh weathered the tempests and tornadoes of the late 1960s at Notre Dame, but the turbulence of those times took its toll. A 1969 Sunday magazine profile in *The New York Times*—the main headline was simply "Hesburgh of Notre Dame"—quoted him as saying doctors worried that his workload and incessant travel were "taking 10 years off my life." He was approaching fifty-two then and finishing his seventeenth year as president. Of course, the prognosis proved unduly dire, as the priest celebrated nearly forty-six more birthdays and served another eighteen years as the university's leader.

By welcome happenstance and a young reporter's blind luck, I watched Father Hesburgh closely during my last two years as an undergraduate. That period—from the fall of 1968 through the spring of 1970—encompassed the most trying months of what Father Hesburgh invariably called "the student revolution." Looking back on those days in 1989, he admitted to me, "It was a monumental case of improvisation."

After spending my entire sophomore year studying in France and knocking around Europe, which included the anything-goes, history-making spring of 1968, I was no stranger to mass protests and anarchistic activities. But what made the return to Notre Dame particularly satisfying was that some feature writing I'd done abroad resulted in offers from the Associated Press and other journalistic outlets to do part-time news coverage of the campus. A "stringer," my unimpressive title, is a freelance contributor who receives payment for individual contributions. Before too long, though, with the high volume of stories about Father Hesburgh and everything else that was happening, AP put me on a monthly retainer and asked if I'd do some additional reporting for a "youth culture" desk the wire service was launching in New York. Heady activity for a twenty-year-old who wanted to write professionally at the end of his school days.

Sorting through the files of articles I phoned in to the AP bureau in Indianapolis, one intriguing story stands out from the others. Dated October 29, 1969, the one-column headline is bold and definite:

**Hesburgh
Considers
Quitting**

The lede reports that the priest-president "refused Tuesday [October 28] to deny rumors that he would like to give up the position." The next paragraph presents a striking direct quotation that reinforces qualms about the future: "'I think I'd be an absolute fool if I didn't think about stepping down,' he said. 'You're constantly in the middle.'"

Part of what's termed "a wide-ranging news conference," Father Hesburgh's statement about leaving the presidency came in response to a question about whether he considered becoming the first occupant of a new, more ceremonial office, university chancellor, which would allow another Holy Cross priest to take over as president. (A chancellorship was never created at Notre Dame; however, the position of provost—the chief academic officer and second-ranking figure in the university's hierarchy—was established in 1970 to lighten administrative responsibilities for the person at the top of the school's organizational chart.)

What's fascinating about the remainder of the dispatch is the variety of nonacademic topics that come up and receive attention. At the time Father Hesburgh was a member of a presidential advisory council about the draft and also chairman of the U.S. Commission on Civil Rights. Both governmental posts elicit quotations, and he's asked his opinion of the Vietnam War, then in its fifth year. "There's not much rationale in staying in there forever," he said. "I think it's high time they [the South Vietnamese] stood on their own feet. We have done a whole lot. I'm not sure we can do any more."

This press conference—and the report about it—brings into bold relief the several different directions in which Father Hesburgh was pulled during this period. Commitments at Notre Dame competed for his attention almost daily with high-level appointments in Washington and elsewhere. The frustration of being "constantly in the middle" became most pronounced in the fall semester of 1968 and the early months of 1969. Whispering about him leaving as the university's leader grew louder as "the student revolution" gained followers who voiced ever-changing demands.

Shuffling through all the clippings I saved (and in almost every case reported), some key moments stand out between late 1968 and the October press conference nearly a year later. For three days in 1968 (November 18 to 20), as many as two hundred students demonstrated against recruiters from the Central Intelligence Agency and Dow Chemical. Thirty protesters forced the CIA representative to leave the Main Building without conducting the scheduled interviews when they blocked his entrance.

From February 5 to 10, 1969, a pornography and censorship conference took place on campus, and a couple of days into it local police raided the screening of one of the movies being shown. The confiscation of the film, the bloodying of students while opposing outside authority on university grounds, and the officers' use of mace in beating their retreat escalated the violence at Notre Dame and seemed to chart a different course for campus disturbances.

On February 17, 1969—just a week after the pornography conference—Father Hesburgh released a tough-minded and unambiguously-worded letter to students and faculty about the consequences of future protesting. Famously called the "fifteen-minute rule," it was the first unequivocal statement by a university president in the United States about dealing with unrest that disrupted the activities of others in a detrimental manner. In blunt, definite language, he wrote, "Somewhere a stand must be made." The sentence that received coast-to-coast attention included these words: "anyone or any group that substitutes force for rational persuasion, be it violent or non-violent, will be given fifteen minutes of meditation to cease and desist." If "force" rather than "rational persuasion" continued beyond a quarter hour, suspension or expulsion would follow.

Besides establishing this rule, Father Hesburgh also adopted a philosophical and personal tone near the conclusion of the lengthy letter:

> No one wants the forces of law on this or any other campus, but if some necessitate it, as a last and dismal alternative to anarchy and mob tyranny, let them shoulder the blame instead of receiving the sympathy of a community they would hold at bay. The only alternative I can imagine is turning the majority of the community loose on them, and then you have two mobs. I know of no one who would

opt for this alternative—always lurking in the wings. We can have a thousand resolutions as to what kind of a society we want, but when lawlessness is afoot, and all authority is flouted, faculty, administration, and student, then we invoke the normal societal forces of law or we allow the university to die beneath our hapless and hopeless gaze. I have no intention of presiding over such a spectacle: too many people have given too much of themselves and their lives to this University to let this happen here. Without being melodramatic, if this conviction makes this my last will and testament to Notre Dame, so be it.

With the letter, Father Hesburgh took a stand and provoked a debate in the media and throughout the public at large. The *New York Times*, *U.S. News & World Report*, and other publications reprinted it, and approximately three hundred newspapers devoted editorials to weighing the pros and cons of the fifteen-minute rule. On February 19 the *Chicago Tribune* devoted its lead editorial ("The Duties of Students") to a long excerpt from the letter, complete with this headnote: "We publish it because of the widespread use of disruptive tactics on the nation's campuses, and because it corresponds so closely to our own views."

In one widely circulated commentary, "Handling the Revolts," academic and syndicated columnist Max Lerner, a close observer of what he termed "the passions of the Republic," complimented Father Hesburgh for "a degree of firmness" rare, if not unique, in confronting campus disorder. Lerner, who in the early 1980s taught as a visiting professor at Notre Dame, builds to a characteristically original assessment of the letter:

> Father Hesburgh has a wickedly quotable style. He would make a better columnist than all of my colleagues and I

put together. But his epigrams aside, what his position comes down to is this: that there is much wrong with America and the world, that there is a new generation of able, alert and socially conscious students like none that has preceded it, that only a small minority of the students are committed to the quiet of a boiler factory and the subtlety of the sledge-hammer approach, that there must be a continuous freedom of communication between all the groups with a stake in the university.

But he adds that a university is a community with a history and a tradition, built up laboriously over the decades, and that it has a style and way of life of its own and a necessity for functioning for all the students and faculty. This cannot be maintained except by civility and rationality on the part of all, including the protesters.

For a young reporter, the pornography conference and the release of the letter within days of each other meant little more than fifteen minutes to study or complete homework during two hectic weeks of trying to keep up with campus news. A note home after the conference—my saintly mother saved every epistle—includes this line: "Between the [Chicago] *Sun-Times* and AP, I figured I made 21 phone calls with article material alone." (These words are scribbled on Western Union Press Message copy paper, a stringer's favorite form of stationery.)

In my reporting notes for a follow-up dispatch about campus reaction to the fifteen-minute rule I discover this quotation from a Notre Dame alumnus in a telegram sent to Father Hesburgh and then shown to me: "This is the best thing you've done since you hired Ara Parseghian." As the football coach since 1964, Parseghian had a record at the time of forty wins, seven losses, and three ties—with one national championship in 1966. In his eleven seasons at Notre Dame, he was the most successful coach during Father Hesburgh's presidency, with his teams victorious in 95 of 116 games and national champs twice.

Nearly two decades after quiet returned to American campuses, I considered writing a magazine article about bygone student days, particularly events of May 1970, and contacted Father Hesburgh to see whether he might be willing to discuss what he called (in several essays he composed) the most difficult time of his presidency. A few days after I sent him a note, his response arrived: "I would be delighted to meet with you regarding campus life during the Spring of 1970. It was a wild time." Indeed.

Listening to the audiotape of the interview over a quarter century later, I find the specificity of recall remarkable for someone engaged in so many different activities during the intervening years. Between the striking of matches to keep his cigar lit, names, incidents, and scenes readily come to him as he answers the questions. His rendering even follows a chronological development. Clearly the period left memories still vivid in the mind of a central participant.

On April 30, 1970, a Thursday, President Richard Nixon announced that the Vietnam War was widening with an "incursion" (his word) into another country, Cambodia. The action quickly inflamed opponents of the war on campuses across the country, and at Notre Dame a protest was scheduled for Monday, May 4, on the Main Quadrangle. Before it started, news arrived of violence on the home front. At Kent State University in Ohio, National Guard members had fired on antiwar demonstrators. Four students, it was later confirmed, were killed.

Looking back, Father Hesburgh identified the invasion of Cambodia as the tipping point in his own thinking about the war. "In my mind I was turning a very wide corner," he admitted. "It was high time to say, 'Get out now, tonight before midnight.'"

The Notre Dame Board of Trustees had their spring meetings on campus the Friday, Saturday, and Sunday after Nixon's announcement about Cambodia. One session was cut short after thirty to forty students repeatedly pounded on the doors where the trustees were gathered. "It had been a horrible weekend," he recalled, describing the shouting and the banging on the doors at the trustees' meeting. "I got back to the Main Building about midnight on Sunday. I thought, if I had any brains I'd go to bed; but not having any brains, I went up to my office. A couple of kids came up and said, 'There's going to be a real blowup tomorrow and you better be ready for it.'"

Later in the night, more students stopped by the president's office—one reporting a rumor that the ROTC building was going to be firebombed. Another came by to tell him that he might be asked to speak at the rally being planned for Monday. Father Hesburgh understood the importance of always keeping lines of communication open, even in the wee hours of the morning, which is often prime time for the student-age population. "About three o'clock, Dave Krashna [the student body president] called to ask if I would talk," Father Hesburgh continued. "I said okay, and I thought I'd better have this one in writing, which I generally don't do. I sat down and wrote out a talk in longhand. It was a program of action to get out of Vietnam and to get people convinced to push for that. I left it on Helen's desk [Helen Hosinski was Father Hesburgh's assistant throughout his tenure as president and did all of his typing] about four a.m., with birds starting to chirp, and went back to Corby Hall [where he lived]."

That morning, even before students started assembling for the rally, word circulated across campus that there would be a call to boycott future classes as a symbolic yet significant statement against the conflict-cum-quagmire. By that Monday a hundred or so colleges and universities were already on strike, a number that exploded to well over four hundred after the deadly incident at Kent State. Moreover, ROTC buildings at about thirty schools were set on fire during that week.

Relying on his freshly typed text, Father Hesburgh, as the first speaker at the Notre Dame protest, took an entirely different tack in front of a crowd approaching two thousand. According to my reporting notes, the wind that afternoon kept lifting his pages from the lectern, making it difficult for him to read. At a critical section near the end, the priest-president posed a question—and immediately answered it. "What do you do? I have no inflammatory rhetoric to offer you. I must tell you honestly that violence here at home is the worst possible reaction to the violence you abhor in Southeast Asia. I must tell you that if the world is to be better than it presently is, you must prepare yourselves, intellectually, morally, and spiritually, to help make it better. Striking classes as some universities are doing, in the sense of cutting off your education, is the worst thing you could do at this time, since your education and your growth in competence are what the world needs most, if the leadership of the future is going to be better than the leadership of the past and present. Good leaders were never born of self-indulgence, or self-pity either."

Father Hesburgh then departed from his prepared remarks to deliver one of the most memorable lines I ever heard him speak: "We are living in an age of midgets. I want you to prepare to be giants."

While standards of acceptable metaphor have changed since 1970, what makes this statement historically important is Father Hesburgh's indirect indictment of high government officials he knew and worked with, including Lyndon Johnson and Richard Nixon. Max Lerner was right about the priest's "wickedly quotable style" and its power to deliver a punch.

Although Father Hesburgh argued against a strike, he struck a chord with many students and faculty by proposing a six-point "Declaration" that called for, among other measures, "the withdrawal of our military forces at the earliest moment" and a commitment "to help work for a better America and a better world in a peaceful and non-violent manner." The most trenchant statement in the Declaration, which he invited the students to sign, came in the fifth point: "Most fundamentally, may we state our deep convictions that our national priorities today are not military, but human. Our nation is unnecessarily and bitterly divided on issues at home and abroad. If the war abroad can be quickly and effectively defused, then we can be united at home in our dedication to justice, to equality of opportunity, and to renewing the quality of American life—a task that will require our best personal efforts and even more of our financial resources than those squandered by us in recent years on a largely frustrating and fruitless venture." Interestingly, the Declaration is signed "T. M. Hesburgh, C.S.C." No first name, no formal title—just the five initials before and after his last name.

After Father Hesburgh finished, Krashna, the student body president, took the stage and, as predicted, advocated a more extreme course of action. He urged his fellow students to "stop, look, and listen—and absolutely say 'stop' to the education we're getting at this time." His call to strike had an immediate impact: attendance was spotty for the late Monday afternoon classes, and more than half the student body boycotted classes the next day.

However, a sizable number of students had also listened closely to what the university's president said, and they hatched a plan of their own. Retelling the sequence of events as the smoke of his cigar started to resemble a mushroom cloud, Father Hesburgh mentioned small details that added flavor and spice to the account. What did he do right after his big oration and Declaration? Well, he strolled over to the barbershop, then located in Badin Hall, for a haircut. After that stop—"It seemed a funny thing to give that talk, which turned out to be a key thing, and then go over and get a haircut"—he walked to the Main Building for his afternoon appointments.

"When I went back to the office," he related, "there were a bunch of young people standing around wanting copies of the talk. I said, 'Sure, how many do you want?' They said, 'Thousands.' I said, 'What do you want all of the copies for?' They said, 'We're going to have students go to every house in town and try to have them sign the program.' I said, 'I'll tell you what: You guys do that, and when you get all of the signatures I'll make sure the president [Nixon] gets them.'"

During the next few days—and largely because Father Hesburgh set the tone and provided the spark—there was not only a mood of seriousness but also an explosion of energy across the campus. Students fanned out through South Bend and Mishawaka, seeking signatures for the "Hesburgh Declaration." Letter-writing campaigns churned out thousands of antiwar missives to the president, members of Congress, American bishops, and news organizations. Discussion groups gathered for what were then called "teach-ins." Students assembled to debate America's proper role in the world and to pray for an end to violence at home and abroad. Outdoor Masses were offered daily, with one for the students killed at Kent State concelebrated by some thirty priests.

Two days after the rally on the Main Quad, the largest march in the history of Notre Dame took place. According to official estimates, upwards of five thousand people wove through the campus and then hiked on South Bend streets to Howard Park near the Saint Joseph River for a community-wide demonstration. However, the mixing of gown and town went well beyond this very visible expression of dissent from the existing war policy. Students kept going door to door in the Greater Michiana region and ultimately collected twenty-three thousand signatures in support of the Hesburgh Declaration.

True to his word, the priest packaged all of the signed pages and delivered them to the White House. In a personal letter to Nixon accompanying the petitions, Father Hesburgh noted,

> The academic community represents about 30% of America and it is important that it has some input into the councils of state. I believe that in general this community is intelligent, generous, idealistic, and dedicated to the best interest of the country. It is also obstreperous, noisy, occasionally violent, almost always critical, but, again, committed to the best that America can be and this commitment far outweighs the negative elements that make the academic community troublesome. I have seen a moral rebirth on this campus during the past ten days of May that is unparalleled in my lifetime, most of which has been spent at universities, mainly this one. This is a resource that America needs and should use.

In the letter, the priest asks Nixon—whom he'd known for nearly two decades and who had appointed him as chairman of the U.S. Commission on Civil Rights—to take note of what the students had done and to respond to them, "not necessarily agreeing with them, but at least acknowledging the fact that they cared enough to make their opinions known and are willing to dedicate themselves to the best interest of our country." Father Hesburgh received no response and never even knew whether the president saw his letter or was aware of the Declaration. But the consequence of public outcry across the nation, together with stiff congressional disapproval, resulted in the withdrawal of U.S. troops from Cambodia by the end of June.

Though Father Hesburgh's vocal and programmatic turn against the war proved decisive for him, he was by no means alone. A few days after the rally on the Main Quad, I typed up a dispatch to send to the Associated Press in New York. One statement by a student I'd interviewed leaps off the Western Union sheet even as I reread it today, not only as a personal comment, but also as a representative reaction to that long-ago time: "Up until Monday, I was sure I wanted to be a chemistry major. Then I found out that a friend of mine had been one of the ones killed at Kent State. I started attending the discussions and teach-ins, and now I'm pretty much convinced that I'll switch my major to something where I'll later have personal contact with people and not science equipment. With everything that happened, it's probably a minor decision, but for me it's the most important thing I can do."

As we talked years later, Father Hesburgh drew a straight line connecting May 1970 and his letter enunciating the fifteen-minute rule. He remarked, "What happened in '70 was the real turning point, but the letter had laid down the ground rules. People were hungry for someone to stand up to the mob and say, 'Okay, this is far enough. We don't go any farther.'

"There had been some pretty rough stuff going on [at other schools]. The one thing that struck me, though, was that our students were different from the others in several aspects. They had an instinctive moral approach; it wasn't just the revolution for the sake of revolution. They really knew that there was a moral dimension to America. I think it's fair to say it's the first time in the history of this country that the young people educated and turned around the older people. It's always been the other way around. They were so convinced, and they were so universally worked up on this.

"The second thing that was important is that whenever we had a real crisis it was almost always tied to the liturgy. Many of our big moments during that terrible period were punctuated by Masses out on the Main Quad.

"The third thing, I think, was that our students were never all that devious. We had a devious small group trying to really cause mischief—maybe not in their minds; I don't want to judge them. They probably had high motives, as all revolution-aries do. But we also had a good, solid core of people who could be convinced otherwise. You could reason with them. If you gave them a decent program that responded to their idealism, they would pick it up and run with it. I didn't insist that they go all over town [with the Hesburgh Declaration]; they did that on their own.

"Well, you put all of those things together and it probably illustrates what I meant by a moral resurgence. This was not just another wild thing like winning a national championship or something. This was something at the heart of the nation and was something that was also tied into other good things like human rights and poverty and racial problems of all kinds. It was kind of a mixed bag, but the bag was definitely a moral bag. The youngsters were right in general. They were right on the war, and they were right on a lot of things."

Remembering this era and sketching out his perspective, Father Hesburgh spoke with a certain amount of personal satisfaction. Yet, as he knew from experiences at other schools during this period, what might happen was then as unpredict-able as Midwestern weather in March. Noting the poignancy of the act, he carried in his billfold a list of the college and uni-versity presidents he knew who had either been driven from office or died as a result of physical ailments exacerbated by the turmoil on their campuses. Remarkably, the number ap-proached two hundred.

Discussing the difficulties he and colleagues faced, Father Hesburgh mused on a question: "Why was it so tough in those days? I said it was so tough because no university president had ever faced this before. There were no rules. There were no set procedures."

The letter with the fifteen-minute rule was one academic administrator's effort to impose a definite regulation on demonstrations or activities that had the potential for exceeding the limits of free speech or assembly. In November 1969, two hundred and fifty protesters demonstrated against recruitment sessions conducted by Dow Chemical Company and the Central Intelligence Agency. Ten students challenged the rule and received a formal warning that suspension or expulsion would result. All ten were ultimately suspended for one semester. In his matter-of-fact way, Father Hesburgh said, "It was tested once, and that was the end of it."

"Ted the Head" was the nickname students back then used most often when referring to Father Hesburgh. In most undergraduate circles he had not as yet become the "Father Ted" of later and common parlance. The image of strong leadership that he projected on campus and through the broadcast media from his frequent appearances made him even more of a public figure and household name than he was before campus unrest began.

Covering so many of his news conferences and speeches, what struck me was his fluency in discussing so many different subjects and the distinctive way he introduced the language of idealism and improvement in explaining earthbound problems. Typically, his eyes would gaze heavenward, as though for divine inspiration, and he would then provide the ins and outs of proposed legislation or the complexities of Church thinking as he looked straight at the reporters and photographers. Before anyone had ever read or heard of the media's attraction to the sound bite, Father Hesburgh understood the importance of the direct, concise, quotable line journalists relish in writing copy or producing broadcast segments.

Besides conveying mastery of his material, he was the very definition of a quick study. That was evident at press conferences and on other occasions. At a home basketball game during my student years, I happened to get a ticket near where he was seated in what was then called the ACC, the Athletic and Convocation Center. As the end of the first half approached, he reached inside his suit coat pocket and extracted a single sheet of paper. He read it quickly, put it away, and when the buzzer sounded to end the half headed to the floor. Without any notes, he stood at half-court and delivered remarks about an award recipient (standing next to him) and the meaning of the award itself.

In public, usually in front of cameras and recording devices of different kinds, Father Hesburgh was the picture of a person in command. Self-assured, ready with a pithy comment, cordial in the give-and-take, both photogenic and telegenic, he always seemed in control—as though he knew every move he might make and had considered every word he would speak.

That image, however, was by no means a true, three-dimensional portrait of who he was and how he felt in dealing with "the student revolution." Near the end of our interview he made a confession about the time and what he had to endure. When I inquired whether it was his most difficult period as president, he quickly responded, "No question about it." Then he laughed and said with more emphatic certainty, "No question whatever. It was an agony. I remember getting up every morning with a knot in my stomach and saying, 'What are they going to do today?' and then 'What am I going to do?' You never knew the answer to either of these, so you went through day by day." A little while later he added a lasting remembrance: "I think I had a perpetual knot for about three or four years. You were always under pressure."

A night owl for office work, even when a crisis wasn't brewing, Father Hesburgh famously met with students in the early morning hours—"I always felt you should be available"—and he wanted to maintain direct access. On occasion, though, the open-door policy could lead to unsettling encounters. "You had to practice a lot of patience, and yet you had to be reasonable," he told me. "I remember very well one night when a big, gangly guy who looked like death warmed over—inordinately thin and gaunt and disheveled—walked into my office, and I was talking on the phone to someone in the wee hours of the morning. I happened to look up from my desk, and there is this guy standing there with a can of beer in his hand. I just put my hand over the receiver. 'Four things for you: Out in the hall. Don't ever come in this office again without knocking, because I wouldn't go into your room in a residence hall without knocking. If you've got something you want to talk to me about, after this personal phone call, I will come out to see you. You can decide if you want to wait or not. So, out.'"

Treacherous as those times were, Father Hesburgh could see their long-term value in shaping the final two decades of his presidency and the years that followed. Dealing with all of the antiwar insurrections and declaring his opposition to hostilities in Southeast Asia had nurtured his own commitment to peace and to the nonviolent resolution of conflict. The "agony" he endured during those up-for-grabs years created, metaphorically speaking, the seedbed for his sustained study and speaking on the necessity for finding ways of avoiding warfare, especially with modernity's weapons.

"You can't go through those experiences without really being terribly concerned about even much larger problems than how to keep peace in the university," he noted. The educator and concerned citizen started to look beyond the borders of one campus to ponder what a university—and he as an individual—might do to help achieve peace in the wider world.

A small first step was the creation of a program dedicated to the study of nonviolence at Notre Dame, which began during the 1969–1970 academic year. The Associated Press saw story possibilities in this novel initiative, and I wrote some articles about it for the wire service. A lengthy feature, distributed in March 1970, noted in boldface (right below the headline) words that still quicken an old scribbler's pulse:

By BOB SCHMUHL
Written for The Associated Press

Immodestly, I collected several copies from different newspapers that ran the story with this lede: "SOUTH BEND, Ind.—The University of Notre Dame's pioneer study of nonviolence, at a time when the New Left is teaching military tactics on some of the nation's campuses, has met enthusiastic student response."

Seven paragraphs into this article about a new academic approach to counter rebelliousness, the young reporter explains the connection between specific activities on the Notre Dame campus and securing financial support to launch this "pioneer study." Father Hesburgh's famous letter of the year before receives attention, yet with an unexpected financial twist:

There has never been a major disturbance on the Roman Catholic university's campus. But after a police raid on a student-sponsored pornography conference at which blue films were shown, the university's president, the Rev. Theodore M. Hesburgh, issued his "15-minute rule."

It set a deadline for students to meditate, then abandon their demonstration when ordered to do so or be treated as trespassers.

Father Hesburgh's hardline policy to stop disruptive demonstrations was credited at least in part with attracting a $100,000 grant from Gulf Oil Corp. to finance the nonviolence program.

The program planted seeds of its own at the university, and Father Hesburgh became a more prominent advocate for peace-building and alternatives to war. Before he left the president's office, he shared his vision in numerous lectures for students, alumni, and the public at large. In some talks he even sketched out ideas for the kind of serious scholarship and courses in peace studies that he thought should be pursued.

One person who listened closely to his views and academic planning during a speech in San Diego was Joan B. Kroc, the widow of McDonald's founder Ray Kroc. From 1985 until her death in 2003, Mrs. Kroc, who became a close friend of Father Hesburgh after that fateful talk, contributed almost $70 million for the establishment and continuing support of the Kroc Institute for International Peace Studies at Notre Dame. Somewhat ironically, the roots of that highly regarded work sprouted in the unlikely soil of the conflict and chaos that had kept the priest's stomach in a "perpetual knot" during an unforgettable era in what he always remembered as "a wild time."

Father Hesburgh celebrating Mass on Notre Dame's Main Quad, as he neared his retirement as president in 1987. Photo courtesy of the University of Notre Dame Archives.

Reverend Father President

The 1970s brought an end to the Vietnam War, the political career of Richard Nixon, and most of the student rebelliousness of the previous decade. The climate on campuses changed. Storms of the sixties became the occasional squall in the seventies. For those ten years I watched Father Hesburgh from a distance while making periodic visits to South Bend, including the commencement ceremony in 1977 that featured President Jimmy Carter's address on human rights.

After finishing graduate school and developing a news literacy program at Indiana University–Bloomington, I returned to Notre Dame in the fall of 1980. What began as a one-year visiting appointment turned into a tenure-track position, but what I remember most vividly about the first semester of teaching was an attempt at humor that failed yet provided an instructive lesson.

In a class called News in American Life, we focused for a few sessions on that year's presidential campaign between the incumbent Carter, a Democrat, and his Republican challenger, Ronald Reagan. I quoted a story then circulating in the press that Reagan had said, "Trees cause more pollution than auto-mobiles." This somewhat shaky scientific hypothesis had prompted one California citizen to decorate an impressive arboreal specimen with a plea: "Chop Me Down Before I Kill Again." Newspapers published photos of the prank, which I displayed.

As an inexperienced faculty member hypersensitive to student reaction, I couldn't read the silence or the absence of facial expressions—no laughter, no smiles, nothing—to the telling of the story. When one of the students stayed after class, I asked him directly about the class-wide lack of response. "You don't understand what ND means," he replied. "ND means 'No Democrats.'"

The Gipper—of Notre Dame lore and Hollywood fame—was winning on a campus that had made a conservative turn, if this one class could be used as a measuring stick. The causes that exploded during the 1960s were now history, and Father Hesburgh could look ahead to his last years as president without constant glances over his shoulder for brewing trouble or mulling the enforcement of a cease-and-desist order.

In the fall of 1982 I started an academic (and religious) ritual with Father Hesburgh that continued for the next four decades. Most notes to him went something like this: Would it be possible for you to offer a few remarks and a prayer at such and such a gathering on such and such a day? He never refused, although early on other obligations or commitments raised warning flags.

For a conference on The Responsibilities of Journalism in late November 1982, we wanted him to talk about ethics and the news media at a luncheon for nearly 150 journalists and educators. His letter—signed "Father Ted" and the first personal communication I received from him—arrived in mid-September and noted, "Since I'll be coming back from

Vienna the day previous, you had better have a stand-by in case something unforeseen should delay me." We recruited a clerical pinch hitter to be ready for possible use, but he ultimately wasn't needed. Father Hesburgh arrived on time and delivered remarks that, I wrote later in a book of the proceedings, "established the atmosphere for moral dialogue which the conference sought to provide."

I remember as though it were yesterday the reaction of conference participants to Father Hesburgh. Well-known journalists, including Edwin Newman, Georgie Anne Geyer, Jeff Greenfield, and Max Lerner, presented papers and mingled with the attendees, but the luncheon speaker seemed like a human magnet, attracting people for a photo, an autograph, a handshake. Longtime journalists, each with a refined sense of skepticism and a practiced manner of maintaining deliberate distance, lingered by the head table to spend a few moments with someone they clearly admired. At age sixty-five, "Hesburgh of Notre Dame," as the title of a CBS *60 Minutes* profile that aired in March 1982 called him, projected a quality of charisma different from a run-of-the-mill celebrity recognized for little more than being known. It was closer to an earned respect for who he was, what he had accomplished, and how he was able to inspire them, as we had just witnessed and felt.

Moreover, Father Hesburgh genuinely enjoyed the company of journalists. Many news people I invited to campus for one reason or another spent time talking to him, and I often tagged along out of curiosity or as a guide. In April 1983, *New York Times* columnist and two-time Pulitzer Prize winner James Reston came to the university to deliver the first Red Smith Lecture in Journalism. Smith, a 1927 Notre Dame alumnus and sports columnist of enduring literary merit, had died the year before, and his alma mater wanted to recognize him beyond the honorary doctorate he was awarded in 1968.

Who better than Father Hesburgh to launch the lecture series with some opening remarks? He knew Smith and Reston and could speak about both of them in a personal way. Interestingly, to honor the lecture's namesake he quoted from a column Smith composed about (in the priest's phrase) "one of my favorite writers"—Damon Runyon. "To say Damon Runyon's death is a loss to his craft would be like saying breathing under water is inconvenient," Smith had written back in 1946 and Father Hesburgh read aloud, continuing, "Perhaps it should not be said there'll never be another like him. There just never has been up to now." After repeating the quotation, Father Hesburgh added, "These words by Red Smith could very well be said about Red Smith, and what his loss meant to his own craft."

To introduce "Scotty" Reston, the university president emphasized the Washington columnist's significance as a preeminent interpreter of public affairs by reading the honorary degree citation Reston had received from Notre Dame in 1980. Eleven years earlier, in a column about the fifteen-minute letter, Reston had referred to "Father Hesburgh's tough assertion of authority at Notre Dame." The columnist refrained from providing the priest's first name or his formal title in the commentary. From the early 1960s onward, Father Hesburgh needed neither for identification in the national media. Often, as noted, he was simply "Hesburgh of Notre Dame."

After inaugurating the Smith Lectureship, Father Hesburgh took a direct interest in its development, especially after Notre Dame alumnus and South Bend native John P. McMeel and Andrews McMeel Universal became the series benefactors. In 2010 I assembled the lectures from the first quarter century of its history in a book, *Making Words Dance: Reflections on Red Smith, Journalism, and Writing.* The volume's dedication reads:

For Rev. Theodore M. Hesburgh, C.S.C.,
Notre Dame's second founder
and consummate *homme engagé*
with admiration and gratitude

From earliest days on the faculty, Father Hesburgh viewed me as that odd, hybrid fellow who was—in equal measure—an academic and a journalist. The Irish intellectual and popular essayist Conor Cruise O'Brien once cracked that the combination meant he had "a foot in both graves." The dual perception, which I have never minded, came into sharper focus during Father Hesburgh's final years as president, as I worked on a book entitled *The University of Notre Dame: A Contemporary Portrait.* Written at the suggestion of then provost Timothy O'Meara, the book's objective was straightforward but far from simple: describe the university's academic development since its founding, with special emphasis on the years since 1952 and on the word *contemporary.* By the time the volume appeared in the fall of 1986 (about six months before Father Hesburgh's retirement), I had interviewed more than 125 administrators and faculty members. Doing the research, I often said, was akin to enrolling at Notre Dame and taking the introductory course of every department in the university. Looking back, the callow author (struggling to keep up on the so-called tenure track as the book took shape) should have scheduled a psychological evaluation before embarking on what the provost advised should be a "portrait" that duly noted recognizable blemishes and institutional crosscurrents.

The most important interview took place on December 11, 1985: it was the first time I sat down with Father Hesburgh for an extended, taped, one-on-one session. The transcript runs over thirty typed pages—much more than was needed for that book but of remarkable value for this one. In our session, Father Hesburgh reflected on both his presidency and his public and religious service in detail and with specificity. His statements provide a detailed oral history of critical years in his life. He also looked ahead to what he might do after moving out of the office, where we were conversing in an intoxicating cigar cloud. Some of the exchanges include informational or explanatory intrusions added for clarity and context.

More than anything, it is an interview with Father Hesburgh on the threshold of retirement, in his own words and at a pivotal moment. For me, as I reviewed the transcript and listened again to the audiotape, it was like opening a time capsule to discover an exit interview with a person leaving a high position after decades of continuous service. "Reverend Father President"—as the Notre Dame president is addressed during commencement exercises—started out by describing the university's reputation and situation in 1952. He then built on that foundation by explaining the school's development—and his—during the previous three decades.

At the beginning of his presidency, Father Hesburgh realized that the way Notre Dame was perceived in the educational community and by the wider public was crucial to creating centers of excellence in teaching and research. "I knew," he said, "that we had to change the image of the place from what was sometimes called a 'football factory' to an academic image, which is what we exist for."

Recalling a series of press conferences shortly after becoming president, Father Hesburgh said, "The first trip I made to the West Coast, out to Los Angeles and north to Seattle and Vancouver, every single press conference we had was totally populated by sportswriters. I asked if they wanted to talk about education. When they said no, I said, 'Well, then this news conference is over.'

"I figured that would never happen again, and it never has. From that time on, I said we're going to talk about education. I'm not going to talk about football. I have never professionally talked about football or any other kind of athletics. Not that I don't think they're important. They are. It's important that they be very good. I don't knock that. Everything we do we ought to do well, but it shouldn't be the central focus of the place, and isn't."

In the early 1950s, the stereotypical view was so one-dimensional that the new university leader was tossed a football at one news conference to use as a prop for a photograph. "They told me to crouch," he recalled, "and assume the hike position. I just said, 'I'm not the coach. I'm the president. If you want to talk liberal arts, I'll talk. Otherwise, no.' They weren't interested, so I left."

Early on, Father Hesburgh understood that advancing the overall academic enterprise required additional resources, and he shared that concern with Rev. Edmund P. Joyce, C.S.C., who began as executive vice president in 1952 and continued in that position throughout the next thirty-five years. Father Hesburgh pointed out that he and Father Joyce, the chief financial officer, faced three distinct yet related problems in their efforts to have the university more highly regarded educationally. "The first problem was we had a miserable operating budget of under $10 million. That needed to be increased about twenty times if we were going to have decent salaries and decent living conditions. That was the first big challenge: how to generate enough money from tuition and from other sources to be able to grow? On top of that, there was a second problem that we needed about a quarter of a billion dollars' worth of buildings. We needed twice as many buildings, square-foot capacity, than we had at that time, mostly academic buildings but many others as well. The third thing was we had an almost nonexistent endowment. The endowment began here in 1920 and took fourteen years to get to $5 million, and it took another seven years to get to $10 million, which is about where we got in. That needed to be greatly increased for the long range. That was the third problem because we had to do the other two first. In fact, we had to do them all together, but we mainly put the emphasis on enlarging the academic budget and getting salaries up, on the one hand, and getting the facilities into place, on the other. And what we could squeeze out for endowment went into endowment.

"The net of it was that the under $10 million operating budget went to $167 million in 1985–86, and the buildings were built and paid for. There is almost no debt on the university, except a little long-range debt, forty years at three percent, which I consider a gift. And the third priority, the endowment, went from under $10 million to the vicinity of $330 to $340 million today, depending on where the market is." Thirty years later, the annual operating budget is just over $1.5 billion, and the endowment totals nearly $10 billion.

The solution of these three problems dramatically changed Notre Dame from 1952 onwards, enhancing the university's academic stature. Comparing Notre Dame of three decades earlier, Father Hesburgh was precise in explaining where things stood: "First of all, when I came here we had a library that was jam-packed with 250,000 books. You couldn't get more in there for love or money. Today we have a library that has a capacity of 3 million books, and it's better than half full. There are about 1.6 million volumes, plus a million items in microfilm or microfiche, including extensive material from Europe's first public library, Milan's Ambrosiana.[1] We had good students in those days, but we have superb students today; seventy percent of our incoming freshmen are in the top ten percent of their graduating classes. Today we have twice as many students and three times as many faculty, which means the faculty-student ratio has improved a great deal. Faculty were being paid at the bottom of the scale then nationally. Now they are at the very top of the scale—the top fifteen or twenty out of three thousand schools. Research then was almost nonexistent. We did over $20 million in 1984–85, with virtually all of it coming with support from the outside; half our proposals are funded. Today's endowment reflects two things I am very proud of. First, we had no endowed professors in 1952. We have over sixty fully endowed today, with twenty more partially endowed. We'll have twenty more to add to that very soon. Before I leave, we hope to have one hundred fully endowed. [In 2016, there are more than 270 endowed professorships and directorships.] Second, we had $100,000 endowed in scholarship money then. We have over $50 million today, with $6 or $7 million for minorities. I hope to have more than $100 million before I get out of here." (There are now 2,145 endowed scholarships at Notre Dame.)

Besides the growth in academic stature and the wherewithal that helped make it possible, Father Hesburgh seemed proud of the different attitude among students that he saw at the end of his presidency. Notre Dame undergraduates and graduates were becoming much more involved in public service

---

1. The Hesburgh Libraries today, including the main Theodore M. Hesburgh Library and nine satellites across campus, contain more than 3.3 million volumes, in excess of 3 million microform units, more than 34,000 electronic titles, and nearly 30,000 audiovisual items.

and leadership roles than ever before. "There's a whole spirit today," he explained. "I don't know how many students back in 1952 were working for the less fortunate. But if there were any doing so, I didn't know about them. Today about a third of our student body is working for the less fortunate, and about ten percent of our graduates are going into such work for a year or two of their lives after they graduate. On top of that we have over three thousand graduates today working in higher education, including about thirty-five presidents of colleges or universities. We have hundreds of priests and sisters and dozens of bishops who have been educated here. We have an astronaut; we have generals and admirals; we have over eight hundred CEOs or senior officers of corporations, large and small, across the land. We have thousands of lawyers (and a growing number of federal judges), as well as thousands of medical doctors. One of them, James E. Muller, was a cofounder of the International Physicians for Prevention of Nuclear War, which won the 1985 Nobel Peace Prize. We have Pulitzer Prize authors.

"I can remember in those days [the early 1950s] people used to say, 'Who are your outstanding graduates?' One would cough and say, 'Well, there is Frank Walker, who was Postmaster General.' Then one might cough again and, if he were fairly liberal, say, 'George Shuster, president of Hunter College.' Then it would stop about there. Knute Rockne might be mentioned or something of that sort, but I can recall very well it was not easy in those days coming up with a distinguished list. Today, we are one of a handful of universities with a statistically significant number of undergraduate alumni in *Who's Who in America*. Outside America, we have the president of a country [José Napoleón Duarte, a 1948 graduate, who served as president of El Salvador from 1984 to 1989]."

Father Hesburgh's thirty-five years in office established a record for the fourteen Holy Cross priests who preceded him at Notre Dame since its founding in 1842. (Rev. Edward Sorin, C.S.C., the school's founder, was president from 1842 until 1865, with his term of twenty-three years ranking second in length of time.) Looking back at his tenure, the longest of any university president in the United States when he retired, Father Hesburgh pointed to two decisions that he considered to have had the most significant consequences—the transfer of governance from the Congregation of Holy Cross to a predominantly lay board of trustees in 1967 and the admission of women as undergraduates in 1972—remarking, "I think those two changes will be seen as substantial enhancements of the quality of life and of academic excellence at the university."

Father Hesburgh never second-guessed either change and talked repeatedly about the value of honoring Our Lady, Notre Dame, by opening the doors of the campus to those of Mary's gender. "Coeducation has had a marvelous effect on Notre Dame," he wrote nearly two decades after the decision. "First and foremost, we had always maintained that we were in the business of educating students for leadership, and now we had broadened that commitment to include the other half of the human race. Almost as important, the women brought their great gift of femininity to our campus. . . . Another facet of coeducation was that with the admission of women we had doubled our source of applicants, and that enabled us to raise our admission standards even higher."

Assessing the early and middle years of his presidency and what he imagined Notre Dame might become, Father Hesburgh commented without hesitation, "It's probably better than I envisioned it might be. We've been very, very fortunate. We've had generous benefactors and first-rate leadership. During this long time I've been president, there have been four or five vice presidents in every one of the sectors, and they have all served with distinction. Some of them burned out by giving all they had. Many people have been involved in the march forward. You tend to get a lot of the credit if you are up at the head of the procession. The fact is that your achievement rests on the efforts of others."

Leadership wasn't complicated, he noted, and in this respect he was following in the footsteps of Theodore Roosevelt, who once remarked, "The best leader is the one who has sense enough to pick good men to do what he wants done, and the self-restraint to keep from meddling with them while they do it." While Roosevelt lived at a time before women had the opportunity for leadership roles in America, Father Hesburgh had, in his time as the university's president, become more inclusive, speaking of "the people" with whom he worked and served as leader.

"The secret," he told me, "is really to get the very best people you can get, even if they are better than you are, and to get them in the right slot. But once you get them appointed to that slot and get their agreement to do the work, then leave them alone. Don't try to second-guess them. Don't try to say who is going to be their assistant and who is going to work with them. That's their problem. I always told them, 'You do your work, and I'll do mine. Whatever you do, you are going to get the credit for it, and whatever you do I'll back you on it. Unless you make an absolute mess of it, I'm with you all the way.'

"As a result, people know that they have their own bailiwick that they are going to run themselves. They are going to pick their people, and they are going to have a reasonable freedom to have their own particular vision within the bigger vision. My responsibility is to have the overall vision, but others have to have goals, too, for a wide variety of things from academics to athletics; to maintaining buildings; to providing security; to making books available; or to having a computing system that works. Administrators who don't make it are fussy administrators who are constantly sticking their noses into other people's business and telling them how to do things. A much better system is to get people who know much more about a specific area than you do and let them go. Again, you also have to make sure that if something good happens they get the credit for it. You can get an awfully lot done if you don't care who gets credit for it. My job, I think, is to see that the person who did it gets the credit for it."

From his general observations about academic leadership, Father Hesburgh focused his attention on one person deserving great credit for having "an integral and important part of advancing the vision of a great Catholic university." Father Joyce had been responsible for all financial matters, and he also served as chairman of what was then called the Faculty Board in Control of Athletics (now the Faculty Board on Athletics) and head of the University Building Committee. Speaking in 1985, Father Hesburgh said, "He and I are quite different. He is very good with numbers, and I'm better with words. He knows finances. I think of other things and hardly ever think of finances directly. I spend money, and he has to raise and conserve it and make sure the balance sheet comes out even at the end of the year. Despite some tough times in the national economy, we have had only one year in the red in thirty-three years. I give him the credit for it because he is in charge of the budget.

"He has brought to Notre Dame everything that I couldn't bring to it. I include our national reputation for an athletic program with integrity. What he does often is kind of invisible, while I'm always giving the speeches and getting my picture taken and being visible. Whatever was accomplished during the last thirty-three or thirty-four years, Ned Joyce deserves credit for a half share of any praise."

Father Hesburgh's visibility extended far beyond the Notre Dame community, principally because of his service to the government, the Catholic Church, and several institutions in the private sector. In one profile, *People* magazine remarked that "while he is a respected figure in academia, his extracurricular (and extra-ecclesiastical) activities have made him a national figure." Named to the National Science Board in 1954 by President Dwight Eisenhower, Father Hesburgh ultimately held fifteen other presidential appointments. He was a charter member of the U.S. Commission on Civil Rights, created in 1957, and he served as chairman of the commission from 1969 to 1972. He was, to use his word, "fired" from this post by President Richard Nixon for his criticism of the Nixon administration's civil rights record. In 1974 President Gerald Ford appointed the priest-educator to be a member of the Presidential Clemency Board, which decided how to deal with the civilians and military personnel accused of violating civilian or military law during the Vietnam War. From 1977 through 1979 Father Hesburgh held the rank of U.S. Ambassador, the first Roman Catholic priest to serve in a formal diplomatic role for the American government. He was appointed by President Carter to lead an eighty-person delegation to the 1979 United Nations Conference on Science and Technology for Development in Vienna.

During the last two years of the Carter administration, Father Hesburgh was also the chairman of the U.S. Select Commission on Immigration and Refugee Policy. The commission (composed of four cabinet members, eight members of Congress, and four other people appointed by the president) advocated new legislation for immigration reform. In 1982 President Ronald Reagan named Father Hesburgh to be a member of the U.S. Official Observer Team for the strife-torn El Salvador elections. What he remembered from that experience was not helicoptering between rural villages to check balloting, but the chance meeting of a funeral cortege carrying a young victim of the country's civil war to burial. The procession lacked a priest. Father Hesburgh comforted the mother of the deceased, blessed the casket in Spanish, and gave the woman a rosary. Participating on the observer team didn't mean he'd neglect what he considered his spiritual duties.

In one capacity or another, Father Hesburgh served every president from Eisenhower through George W. Bush. He also received appointments from four popes. From 1956 until 1970, at the request of Pius XII, John XXIII, and Paul VI, Father Hesburgh was the permanent Vatican representative to the International Atomic Energy Agency in Vienna. In 1972 Pope Paul VI asked Father Hesburgh to create the Ecumenical Institute for Advanced Theological Studies in Jerusalem, and Pope John Paul II named Father Hesburgh to the Pontifical Council for Culture in 1983.

In addition to his service to the government and to the Church, Father Hesburgh was also actively involved in organizations in the private sector while serving as Notre Dame's president. He was appointed to the board of trustees of the Overseas Development Council in 1971, and he chaired the council, which assisted people living in the developing world, from 1971 until 1982. In 1979 and 1980 he served as cochairman of the Cambodian Crisis Committee, a group that raised some $70 million to avert mass starvation in Cambodia. He was the first priest to be named a trustee of the Rockefeller Foundation, and he was on its board of trustees from 1961 until 1982, the last six years as the chairman. He was also the first priest to serve on the board of directors of the Chase Manhattan Bank. He practiced what he told others: "Anyone who refuses to speak out off-campus does not deserve to be listened to on-campus."

Of all of his activities outside the university, Father Hesburgh considered his experience on the U.S. Commission on Civil Rights the most challenging and yet the most rewarding, saying, "We literally changed the face of the nation. We took a three-hundred-year-old geographical apartheid and eliminated it in 1964 with the omnibus Civil Rights Act. Then we changed for all times voting patterns, when six million blacks were given the vote in 1965. With the entry of blacks into the state schools in the South; with the dismantling of legally mandated separate education for all black youngsters in the South; with the opening up of equal job opportunity; with a dramatic change in the all-white administration of justice; with the total elimination of de jure prejudice—that had to be the high point of my federal service."

In the private sector, Father Hesburgh thought his years on the Rockefeller Foundation were of landmark significance for agriculture and education in developing countries. "We sponsored the Green Revolution that saw six times as much food produced on the same land and by the same farmers. World hunger lingers as a massive problem, but it would be a lot worse without the Green Revolution. We had more ships on the sea bringing food to India during Lyndon Johnson's presidency than were going across the English Channel on D Day. Today, India is exporting food because of the Green Revolution. The same would be true of many other countries in the Orient. We also spurred education throughout the Third World through a $150 million program. Some of the universities have not developed as quickly as we would have liked, but at least that was a beginning."

Incredibly, though he was so active away from Notre Dame, Father Hesburgh refused ten invitations to outside appointments for each one he accepted. He turned down the chance to be the administrator of NASA under President Johnson as the Apollo program's mission to the moon was developing; he declined an offer from President Nixon to become director of the War on Poverty, and he said no to President

Carter's invitation to be the State Department's chief official on Latin American affairs. Overtures to run for public office were also turned aside. "I always refused to do something unless I could do it wholeheartedly as a priest and as a person in higher education. I felt those were my two tasks in life, and I didn't want to get distracted." Warming to the subject, he offered a more detailed explanation for exactly how he made decisions about agreeing to do work in the public sphere: "I decided early on that I wouldn't ever want to run for an elective office, because that separates people, one party from another. If you belong to one party, you alienate everybody in the other party. I felt being a priest unified people and didn't divide them. For the same reason, I never endorsed a political candidate. I never have.

"I would serve the public on appointment, if it had some relationship, as I mentioned earlier, to being a priest, which means a spiritual endeavor with spiritual implications—such as foreign aid to poor countries or civil rights. It also couldn't be incompatible with being president of the university. By and large, I think I've hewed close to that line, although I have passed up a lot of interesting jobs in the process."

Despite the sharp distinctions he enforced about his service, Father Hesburgh remained a very active citizen at the same time that he led Notre Dame. "I sat down the other day," he recalled as we talked, "and figured that I had spent forty-seven years on public service, probably more than that on private service during these years in the presidency, albeit part-time work. But some of that part-time work meant thirty or forty days a year, and that's a pretty big chunk of a year. It's more than you get for vacation. I went around the world many times during those activities, twice just during that activity of being an ambassador under Jimmy Carter for using science and technology for world development."

These outside appointments made Father Hesburgh realize that as he served as president he juggled several jobs simultaneously. He heard criticism that he might be overly involved beyond Notre Dame, but rejected the grousing. In a 1986 interview for the book *"What Works for Me": 16 CEOs Talk about Their Careers and Commitments*, he commented, "Some people would say that I've squandered myself by spending so much time on outside jobs, but I'd say that I've enriched myself and Notre Dame as well."

Explaining his approach as a chief executive officer with several other high-level tasks, Father Hesburgh noted that he worked "double shifts" when he was on campus and followed a basic philosophy for managing his time. "When I have done something, it is over," he said. "I don't worry about what I said or how I said it. I do the best I can while I am doing it, and so be it. There are a zillion things in between, so paying real attention to each thing as it comes along is important. It is just as important to learn to wipe out what just happened. Let what's coming next be your focus of attention."

Despite the diversity of the many different activities, Father Hesburgh told me he discerned a unifying pattern to all of them. As a priest-educator, he always sought "to see the Kingdom of God spread throughout the world. I think the Kingdom of God in our age may spread faster through education and development activities than through other activities." Moreover, Father Hesburgh saw a relationship between his outside endeavors and his work as university president, notably in such areas as science, human rights, and economic development. "Those outside experiences are all reinforcing; you establish a national—in fact, a worldwide—network. A lot of the work overlapped, intensifying my own education and giving me ideas about intellectual inquiries Notre Dame ought to foster. Human rights overlap with world development; that overlaps with food problems around the world, the Green Revolution; that overlaps with university development of the Third World, and so on."

All of Father Hesburgh's involvement in service beyond education created a new ethos at Notre Dame: active engagement in organizations and projects to help others, including those less fortunate. (He once wrote, "We teach human dignity best by serving it where it is most likely to be disregarded, in the poor and abandoned.") He found the commitment of an increasing number of students, faculty, and alumni to volunteer work deeply satisfying.

As other people donated their time and talents, they were, in a way, a reflection of the busy person in the president's office. Father Hesburgh's example was influential in opening the door for off-campus endeavors to benefit men and women not only near the university but also nationally and internationally. That spirit of service extended well beyond Father Hesburgh's retirement in 1987 and endures today in programs for both students and alumni.

His active participation in off-campus activities also tangibly enhanced the resources for research at Notre Dame. Papers, reports, and books related to his public, private, and religious service are now available at the university for use by scholars. In fact, as a result of his years of service on the Commission on Civil Rights and on the Select Commission on Immigration and Refugee Policy, Notre Dame houses one of the most comprehensive archives on civil rights and immigration in the United States.

Beginning in the early 1980s, Father Hesburgh significantly reduced his responsibilities outside the university to devote as much time as possible to doing what he could to combat "the nuclear threat to humanity." Though interested in the subject for decades, he became alarmed in 1981 about the possible use of nuclear weapons. "It suddenly struck me—I knew it all the time, but there is a difference between knowing something and being struck by it—that everything else that I've been working on all my life would literally be wiped out by a nuclear attack. It would be the end of everything. It would be the end of all the great institutions, such as the universities, governments, libraries, and families. Everything would be gone. Our future would be gone and with it everybody else's future—the future's future, if you will. If we don't solve this problem, the rest of our problems simply become irrelevant. Without human beings you don't even have the concept of problem."

The realization that the planet itself was in jeopardy had a profound impact on Father Hesburgh. "When that conviction really hit me hard," he recalled, "I decided that I would get out of everything else and get into this problem. I didn't get out of education or a few things that I just couldn't get out of without them falling apart. So I stayed with the things I absolutely had to stay with, but tried to go as full-time as I could on this. Not just doing anything, but doing what I felt my past life prepared me to do."

In this realm, Father Hesburgh sought to bring together representatives of the world's religions and noted scientists from the five major nuclear powers, including the United States and the Soviet Union. As we talked he described the project as the intellectual and interdisciplinary convergence of representatives from the two realms of science and religion. "Scientists fashioned the nuclear monster, and they bring that credibility to the discourse," he remarked. "Religious leaders have a moral standpoint. To facilitate the conversation we began by setting up a program for peace studies in Jerusalem."

In December 1985, the same month as my extended interview with Father Hesburgh, he received on behalf of Notre Dame a $6 million gift from Joan Kroc to create the Kroc Institute for International Peace Studies. The benefactor and the recipient were both committed to peace, justice, and studying the causes of violent conflict, including how to reduce or even eliminate the threat of nuclear arms.

Father Hesburgh saw his previous experience, both inside and outside the university, as appropriate preparation for becoming involved in seeking peace, and he identified the pursuit of peace as central to his plans for his post-presidency years. As with his earlier activities, this effort fulfilled his mission as a priest and educator. Interestingly, as we talked, he singled out his vocation to the priesthood—after theological studies in Rome he was ordained in Sacred Heart Church at Notre Dame in 1943—as the principal stimulus for engaging in such a varied life.

"I can't remember a time when I didn't have about ten concurrent jobs," he said, but identified a sense of unity that came from being a priest. "I offered Mass every morning or at night or whenever I could do it when I had time. When you're traveling you can't always control your time, but I said Mass every day except once, when I was stuck in a hospital. Secondly, I said my breviary every day. I thought it was a bit of a drag when it was said in Latin, but now that it's in English, I find it a delight. I've also probably said the rosary almost every day. I've never passed up a chance to be a priest and anything that might involve. It often involved counseling, or talking to people, or helping people in the unique way that you can as a priest, sacramentally or otherwise. I think that's the common thread that kept me going, and I simply cannot view my life apart from being a priest, whether it's my past life or my future life. I don't really want to be anything else.

"There were a couple of times that I could have been a bishop [Pope Paul VI had even hinted at the possibility of becoming a cardinal, Father Hesburgh told me years later], but I felt at the time what I was doing and the demands that had to be met, couldn't be met if I didn't keep at them, so I didn't think that was much of a temptation. I've been far enough on the fringes at times—probably that temptation has been removed permanently from my life."

Even with the crowded schedule of activities and travels he maintained after joining the Notre Dame faculty in 1945 as an assistant professor of religion—he received his doctorate in sacred theology from the Catholic University of America earlier that year—and becoming executive vice president in 1949, Father Hesburgh wrote several monographs and came out with two books during his time in the presidency. Some of his most important lectures and essays are included in *The Humane Imperative: A Challenge for the Year 2000*, published by the Yale University Press, and *The Hesburgh Papers: Higher Values in Higher Education*, published by Andrews and McMeel.

Father Hesburgh's work inside and outside education during his presidency brought considerable recognition to him and to Notre Dame. In 1984 the university awarded him an honorary doctorate, his one hundredth. In 1964 President Johnson bestowed on him the Medal of Freedom, the nation's highest civilian honor. He received the Alexander Meiklejohn Award from the American Association of University Professors in 1970, recognizing his outstanding contribution to upholding academic freedom. In 1982 he won the Jefferson Award, given by the Council for Advancement and Support of Education, for his leadership in the field. More than fifty different national and international organizations gave him special awards between 1952 and his retirement.

In leaving the president's office, Father Hesburgh didn't plan to curtail his involvement with the university. "Notre Dame has been my whole life," he said, "and I'm certainly willing to do anything I can do. But I don't want any job that has any line authority going with it. I don't want a position or a title, except that I suppose that academic tradition would anoint me president emeritus. I don't want anybody sitting where I'm sitting now, thinking he's got to use me, or that I'm an anchor around his neck, or that I'm a rival of his in some way."

From his first days as president of Notre Dame, an abiding vision animated Father Hesburgh. That vision—the creation of a great Catholic university—came closer to reality during his tenure. Describing what he sought to do, he combined abstract principles and concrete conditions: "I've always said without equivocation that I want it to be a great university that is also a great Catholic university. That's a dual goal. It's much easier to be a great university than to be a great Catholic university. It's no great secret how to become a great university, if you can get the resources for it. You have to have an intellectually curious student body, an intellectually competent faculty, and classrooms, laboratories, museums, and libraries where they can get together.

"But a great Catholic university goes beyond that. We need people who have a commitment to the philosophical and theological implications of all the great questions of our times. We need people who inquire about transcendentals and not just temporary things. We need people who are concerned with the moral and the spiritual as well as the intellectual formation of students. You have to have people who can speak to values and whose life professes them. Such teachers are rare, and that is why becoming a great university is easy compared to becoming a great Catholic university."

At the end of our interview, I told Father Hesburgh that I would give him a draft of what I wrote so he could revise or amend the quotations, a practice I was following with each section of the book about contemporary Notre Dame. Without a pause, he said, "That's not necessary. I trust you."

A first-time author worries full-time just before and right after a book's publication. What will the reactions and reviews be like? How do the people involved assess the finished product? Who might be miffed for one reason or another?

As it turned out, Father Hesburgh gave me an inscribed copy. The note above his photo began, "Autographing this for you is really carrying coals to Newcastle. It's your book." Later I learned that he signed some three hundred copies that his office distributed to his friends and university benefactors. To me he also sent a cordial follow-up letter, commenting specifically on his profile and the completed volume: "The whole book is just what we have long needed," he wrote. "I am sure it will be useful for many years to come, and then you can write a new one bringing it up-to-date."

Once his letter arrived, I stopped my authorial fretting and turned to other career-related anxieties. When the book appeared in the fall of 1986, I was also coming up for evaluation in the make-or-break (some might say life-or-death) tenure review process at Notre Dame. Near the end of that semester, the telephone rang, and a senior editor at *Sports Illustrated* inquired whether I'd consider writing on a full-time basis for his magazine. This out-of-left-, right-, or centerfield possibility caused a certain amount of consternation for someone who had cut his journalistic teeth as a sportswriter.

A tenure decision is always chancy, and the offer from *Sports Illustrated* was definite—with an early 1987 start date. However, since I had already spent several years trying to do the kind of teaching and research Notre Dame expected of a junior faculty member, I was reluctant to toss all that aside in haste for a job distinctly different from an academic one. The temptation of moving to New York to write full-time was seductive, but a possible career and life at Notre Dame possessed a stronger, more deeply rooted hold.

The final group of faculty to whom Father Hesburgh awarded tenure and promotion was announced in May 1987, just before he officially retired on June 1. That list, thankfully and praise every saint, included my name. The bet with myself about future employment—the unknown vs. the known—paid off. Three decades later, I have no regrets, and Father Hesburgh played a role in my time at Notre Dame during almost every one of those years.

Father Hesburgh and President Jimmy Carter meet in the White House on August 14, 1979, prior to the United Nations Conference on Science and Technology for Development. Father Hesburgh served as U.S. Ambassador to the conference, the first time a priest ever held the rank of ambassador. Photo taken by White House photographer and courtesy of the University of Notre Dame Archives.

THREE

White House Memories

Father Hesburgh held a deep and abiding civic reverence for the American presidency. Whether the White House occupant was a Democrat or a Republican made no difference to this avowed political independent. If an invitation arrived to serve on a presidential-level board or commission—and it made sense to him as a priest and educator—he almost always answered the call.

His experiences in Washington and elsewhere later became stories that he enjoyed telling to friends, visitors, students, and others. Since I scribbled scores of newspaper columns and magazine articles about the presidency and this country's politics, I never tired of his reminiscences about Dwight Eisenhower, Lyndon Johnson, or Jimmy Carter.

Incredibly, Father Hesburgh met and, in most cases, worked with every president from Harry Truman through Barack Obama. That translates into a dozen of the seventeen chief executives who led the United States during the priest's lifetime. From the 1950s through the early 2000s Father Hesburgh held, as already noted, sixteen different appointments originating at 1600 Pennsylvania Avenue. Some were mentioned in the previous chapter, but here, thanks to the Notre Dame Archives, is the complete list:

Member, National Science Board
Member (and later chairman), United States Commission on Civil Rights
Member, United States Advisory Commission on International Educational and Cultural Affairs
Member, President's General Advisory Committee on Foreign Assistance Programs
Member, President's Commission on an All-Volunteer Armed Force
Member, Presidential Clemency Board
Member, State Department Policy Planning Council
Board of Consultants, National War College
Member and Chairman, Board of Visitors, United States Naval Academy
United States Ambassador, U.N. Conference on Science and Technology for Development
Member, President's Commission on the Holocaust
Chairman, Select Commission on Immigration and Refugee Policy
Member, U.S. Official Observer Team for El Salvador Elections
Member, Commission on United States–Latin America Relations
Board of Directors, United States Institute of Peace
Member, Commission on Presidential Scholars

During spring 2008 I taught a course, American Political Life, that focused on the presidency and the nominating contests in the two parties before that fall's election. By chance, the class met in the auditorium of the Hesburgh Library, and the library's namesake had agreed earlier that semester to partici- pate in a conversation for the students. Almost ninety-one at the time, he planned to talk about his involvement with presi- dents and, more broadly, the nature of presidential leadership.

Like the extended interview we had conducted just before his retirement in 1987, this one looked back over his years of service. On this occasion, though, the class would listen in— and then have the opportunity to ask questions.

During the seventy-five-minute session, which was video- taped for NDtv under the direction of Robert Costa, then a senior at Notre Dame and now a *Washington Post* political correspondent, Father Hesburgh told several stories from an insider's perspective. For instance, in explaining how Lyndon Johnson single-mindedly pursued the passage of the Civil Rights Act of 1964, the "Padre" (LBJ's favored way of referring to Father Hesburgh) even imitated the president's thick Texas drawl, mesmerizing many in the audience. Other memories proved just as vivid and engaging.

The passages that follow are Father Hesburgh in his own words: first about the institution that meant so much to him and then on specific experiences with presidents and their staffs. To avoid repetition or the infelicity inherent in off-the- cuff expression, the quotations are edited, here and there, for continuity and coherence.

Do presidents have common characteristics or traits?

I think the presidents are generally not provincial the way that a congressman would be. Most congressmen are interested in their own districts, whether they are going to get a federal fac- tory or some airfield. Presidents have to think not only of the whole country but also its relationship to the whole world. While some presidents are better at this worldview, some are even better at the national view than others. The fact is that it is terribly important that they stay on top of the national and international picture because that is their job. If they don't do it, there are few other people who can do it. Generally speaking, I think most presidents that I have known have been interested in the world and, of course, interested in their own national problems.

Are presidents intellectual?

You can't really generalize on that, because I would say they were all very intelligent or they wouldn't be where they were. But they are intelligent in different ways. Some were very pragmatically intelligent, in the sense that Lyndon Johnson knew how to get things done in Washington, whereas Jimmy Carter had a dream about what the United States should be, what kind of country it ought to be, what kind of humanistic views it might have. And Dwight D. Eisenhower was just like somebody's grandfather. He oversaw the whole deal nationally and internationally and was just a very nice guy. They are all quite different in their own way, but I didn't have any of them that I would say I didn't like. I had a few bad words with some of President Nixon's associates, but none with him directly. He was always very good to me.

Which presidents impressed you the most?

They impressed me in different ways. I liked Eisenhower because he had a worldview. After all, he had been commanding the greatest army that ever existed, a worldwide army in World War II. He was a broad-gauged sort of fellow. I remember when I invited him to come to Notre Dame to get an honorary degree [in 1960]. I said, "Mr. President, it is great that you can come."

He said, "Since I was a kid in Kansas, I wanted a degree from Notre Dame, and of course I had no way of getting it because I was a poor kid and my family didn't have any money so I went to West Point on an appointment. I went the military route to get educated."

"Well," I said, "you did pretty well." But he was a kind of humble guy, even though he knew the world forwards and backwards. On top of that he was like everybody's grandfather, as I've said.

With which president did you have the closest association?
Well, it's hard to say. I liked them all. I've got to say that they are all different. I liked Eisenhower probably best in one way. He was very good. He came here to get an honorary degree and gave a wonderful talk, and he was also interested by the fact that the priest I got on that occasion was the cardinal from Milan [Giovanni Cardinal Montini], who later became Pope Paul VI. When I met Eisenhower in Gettysburg, he mentioned, "I see where my classmate did well in the election." I answered, "Yeah, he became Pope."

Jimmy Carter to this day is a very good friend of mine. Lyndon Johnson couldn't have been nicer. He gave me the highest award of the U.S. government, the Medal of Freedom, which you have to get at the White House. The first recipient was George Washington, so it's not exactly dog meat.

I have to honestly say I liked them all. I liked some of them a little better, but they were all in their own way guys who had a job to do, and if you helped them do it, they always appreciated it.

Which president asked you to do the most work for him?
I think Carter. He made me U.S. Ambassador for Science and Technology, which is not bad. I ran a three-week international

conference in Vienna after three years on that job, and we accomplished some good things for food in the world and building up the underdeveloped countries of the world. I traveled around the world a couple of times at that job. I was one of the first ones into China.

Freedom is a great thing. Working with the federal government, you can be free if they've asked you to do something, as they did with civil rights, but I felt that the last thing I wanted to do was to get into a political situation as a priest. Everything I did had something to do with humanity, whether it was food for the world, or better citizenship, or better agriculture, or world peace, or peaceful use of atomic energy, things like that. A priest ought to be interested in those kind of things, and it's a moral issue.

Did you ever entertain the thought of running for vice president or any other elected office?
No, but I have to honestly tell you I had offers. But when I became a priest, I decided that the one thing I was not going to do was become a political priest. I wasn't going to be a priest who would run for office, senator or congressman. I knew I could have been elected to either of those jobs. But it seemed to me that, being a priest, you are totally dedicated to the Church and to the people of God, and that gets somewhat mixed up when you are a member of the government and you've got civil authority over people. I don't mind having spiritual authority over people, but you can't mix that up.

Personally, I don't really think it's proper for a priest, especially a priest involved in higher education, to be running for office. I just told people, "Because I am a priest, I think I am making myself ineligible to get involved in a political office." But I am perfectly free as a priest to take on sixteen presidential jobs in Washington and be chairman of some without any problems at all. I could do that kind of thing as a priest without any problem at all because a priest is always kind of an ambassador for the good. So the answer is no. I had a chance, but I would never take the opportunity.

You served on the U.S. Commission on Civil Rights during four administrations, and President Eisenhower made the original appointment.

Yes, he did. That was 1957. I remember it very well because every September I had to go to Vienna for the International Atomic Energy Agency [as the Vatican's permanent representative from 1957 to 1970]. I helped establish that. I helped write the charter, and every September I had to go for the general conference. I remember as I came up the street there was a kiosk, and I noticed a new *Time* magazine. When you are in Europe for several weeks, you really miss what's going on at home, so when I saw this new magazine I bought it right away. Waiting for the light to change, I started to flip through it. When I was flipping through from back to front, I came across a full-page article on the fact that the week before—after arguing for most of June, July, August, and September and filibustering—they finally passed the Civil Rights Act of 1957, which boiled down to the fact that they created a commission to see what the problem was and what the U.S. should do about it: achieving civil rights for all Americans. I said to myself, "It would be just my luck to get on that commission."

I got back home, and a week later on a Sunday afternoon I got a call from the White House. "President Eisenhower wants to know if you will accept an appointment to the U.S. Commission on Civil Rights." I said, "It is a very important subject, and I have been interested in it all my life and, of course I will take the appointment." Then he called me back about five minutes later and said, "I forgot to ask you if you are a Republican or a Democrat." And I said, "Neither. I am an independent." "We will make you a Republican because the commission has to have three of each party, six members, three Republicans and three Democrats. We already have three Democrats, so we will make you a Republican." I said, "Make me anything you want, but I am still an independent."

So, as the complexion of the commission changed over the next few years, I became a Democrat or whatever would fit. It struck me that that commission was going to have a very important role to play. But it was really a bugout on the part of the Congress. Civil rights were such a contentious issue, and then of course it involved the South particularly because of slavery.

The blacks in America were emancipated by Lincoln, but the fact is that for all practical purposes they were not equal as American citizens to white citizens. They had lousy education, which was normally segregated from white education. In the South they spent eight times more per student on whites than they did on blacks. You can imagine what that meant in the way of black education. In the North it wasn't a heck of a lot better, although there was no real differentiation in the budget.

The country had a real problem. We were told to just see what had to be done to solve it. It was almost an insoluble problem because it has been around a long, long time.

I might back up for a moment. When Jefferson, one of our great writers, wrote the Declaration of Independence, it started out, "We hold these truths to be self-evident, that all men are created equal, that they are endowed by their Creator with certain unalienable rights, that among these are life, liberty, and the pursuit of happiness." When he wrote those words "all men are created equal" and endowed with "life, liberty and the pursuit of happiness," it happened that we had Americans who were slaves [nearly 700,000, according to one estimate]. He certainly wasn't writing about them.

Now you fast forward from Jefferson to Lincoln, and Lincoln was a terrific president but really caught up in one of the terrible things a country can be afflicted with, which was the Civil War. It was obvious that as the war cranked up it was about slavery. And at one point, I guess, Lincoln decided it was high time he said something since the fact is that we were not addressing the problem. We were fighting each other, North and South, and it was all about slavery.

Human beings who happened to be white owned other human beings who were black—who had no rights whatever, who worked dawn to dusk, who got no pay for it, who lived in shacks while the whites lived in mansions. They had no civil rights. They couldn't vote; they got no education whatever. It was a pretty awful thing, but it was a picture of what America was when Lincoln became president, and it took enormous courage on his part. But one day he sat down, and he wrote something he called the Emancipation Proclamation, which was to say what this war was really about because no one had come out and said what it was really about. He published the Emancipation Proclamation, and of course he got killed for it. While slaves were free they were still living in those shacks, they were still working dawn to dusk, they were getting paid pennies. They had no education set up at all, and life went on pretty much the way it had in the past, except they were free. None of them ever voted, none of them ever got educated, with a few exceptions here and there.

By the time I became president of Notre Dame in 1952, we had pretty much the same situation that existed after the Emancipation Proclamation. Blacks in this country were free—but they were uneducated, they were untutored, many of them were unemployed because they were uneducated.

It was a pretty dicey thing. That is why they argued [in Congress] all summer long [in 1957], and of course the Democrats were mostly from the South in those days so they had a terrific filibuster going, and finally it did come to an end because it had been about four months, and they were getting no business done at all. They finally did what they always do when they can't find a solution in Washington. They established a commission to solve the problem because *they* couldn't solve the problem. So, out of the blue, we now have the U.S. Commission on Civil Rights, and we had only one power. We could subpoena any American citizen, up to and including the president, to show up and testify under oath on how they stood on human rights for all Americans. It sounds like a small power, but it was actually a fantastic power. The day came later on, when I was chairman of the commission, where I had to subpoena the attorney general, Mr. John Mitchell, who was working for Nixon, and I told him to show up and testify on human rights in Washington, where we were having a hearing. His secretary called my secretary and said he [Father Hesburgh] must be out of his mind expecting the attorney general to go up and testify at an open hearing on civil rights, and my secretary said it is kind of simple. If he doesn't show up, he is going to go to jail. And it's going to be kind of tough putting the attorney general of the United States in jail for not upholding civil rights. Well, he showed up, but he didn't make very good testimony. He was the worst witness we ever had.

But getting back to the story. We met in Washington, and we had this fantastic job of doing something about what had been a perennial problem since the time of Jefferson and Lincoln, and we had to somehow change the course of American history to show that that condition would be changed forever and written into the Constitution, either by law or by amendment to law. We were able to accomplish that role, but it wasn't easy. We had hearings all over the United States. We could go to Miami, San Francisco, Washington, DC, New York, or Chicago and put together a list of people that were important at achieving civil rights, and we had told them they had to come and testify. They either did or went to jail, so they all did it.

But the fact is we were able to go anywhere in the United States and the territories; we even had to work in Samoa and the South Pacific. I had to travel out there on this problem, but (to make a long story short) eventually we proposed a law to correct the problem that we inherited from slavery. Black citizens couldn't exercise their rights equally to have education, housing, voting. They were practically nonexistent politically, and we were supposed to clean up that whole problem.

Well, easier said than done, but I can remember very well when push came to shove, and we were thrown out of Louisiana because the governor and the federal judge there said that the law that created us was invalid and therefore we couldn't come and have a hearing and bring to light all the practices in Shreveport. Well, that went to the Supreme Court, and of course we were upheld and that guy was told he was completely out of order. The law was established, and we went on to do our job, but it was a tough fight all the way. Gradually, by having hearings in Washington, New York, Chicago, San Francisco, Miami, and Dallas, we eventually came up with a picture of what life was like for minorities. These were not just blacks, but it was also increasingly a problem for Mexican Americans. And there were of course many other people whose rights were abused for some reason or another because they were young, or because they were not represented properly, or uneducated, or whatever.

But we persistently had our hearings, and we finally came up with what we thought were a set of laws that would correct the problem. And we covered everything. We covered the civil things like voting, education, housing, employment, the administration of justice, and public accommodations. We decided there was no point in trying to come up with intermediate laws, so we came up with a law that really would cover all of the irregularities we had found out in our hearings across the United States. We came up with the U.S. Commission's Civil Rights Act and sent it to the president and Congress. Eisenhower was going out of office, and the last thing he needed was a big controversy, so he passed it on to the Kennedys. I say the Kennedys because Jack and Bobby operated like a team. Bobby was attorney general, although he had never practiced law. [Father Hesburgh presented Notre Dame's Laetare Medal to President Kennedy in the White House on November 22, 1961, two years to the day before his assassination in Dallas.]

They inherited this problem, and they shoved it to the back burner, and we said, "Why aren't you moving on our proposed law?" They said, "Well, the problem is largely in the South," which was not true; it was a national problem. "If we try to pass a civil rights law, all the southern senators and representatives won't vote for it, plenty of people in the North won't vote for it, and besides it will get us caught up in turmoil, so there is no way on earth we can get that law passed." So it went to the bottom drawer. They did eventually come up with a civil rights law of sorts, but it wasn't the one we wanted.

They never got a chance really to lay it out because, of course, Jack was killed after being in office three years, and in November of the third year [1963] Johnson became the new president. No one ever expected Johnson to be president. The only reason the Kennedys put him in as vice president is because they needed the southern votes to get elected because in those days most of the Democratic party voters were in the South. That's how they got elected [in 1960], and of course the last thing they wanted to do was turn off the South or they never would have gotten reelected. One thing about all prospective presidents: when they walk into that Oval Office, they like to be there for eight years, *not* four years. The way you can guarantee you wouldn't be there for eight years is to come out strongly on civil rights, and you would really get murdered in the next election.

Well, that was the situation when suddenly the president is shot, and Johnson, the Southerner, who had been majority leader of the Senate and knew everything about every lawmaker in Washington, became president. He had a notebook with all of his notes about each one of them, and he is suddenly president of the United States by accident. He really had nothing to lose, but I give him credit for the fact he decided he was going to take on the toughest problem in the history of the United States, which was the problem of race as it goes up against the concept of equality for all American citizens, equal rights for all. So I guess Johnson decided, "If I am going to be known as a good president, I've got to do something," and he decided what he was going to do was to get equal rights for black Americans, Mexican Americans, and other foreign Americans—but really the problem at that point was black Americans. So we were delighted to know that we finally had a president who wasn't trying to avoid the problem. He was going to push for it.

The first week of January [January 8, 1964], Johnson called the Senate and the House to meet [for the president's first State of the Union address]. He comes in with a folder in his hand, and he says, "Ladies and gentlemen, I just want to tell you, you are all going to pass my law." He takes the folder, and he slams it down on the table. What was inside it was the law that we had proposed as a commission to answer all of these problems—to take care of voting, housing, administration of justice, employment, the works. [Johnson's own words: "Let this session of Congress be known as the session which did more for civil rights than the last hundred sessions combined."]

Well, they had all gotten a copy, of course, of our proposed law, and they had all shoved it into the bottom drawer.

But here's a guy now, who is the president of the United States, and he said, You are all going to vote for *my* bill, because now it has become *my* bill. And everybody said, He is out of his mind. This problem has been around since Jefferson and Lincoln, and there is no way on earth this is going to be solved by one guy in Washington. But they underestimated Johnson, and for the next six months he was on the phone every night. He had his little book with all of their foibles, and by all of them I mean senators and congressmen. What he didn't know about them, he could pick up from J. Edgar [Hoover, FBI director], who loved to come to the White House for a scotch at eleven o'clock at night and fill the president in about some things he didn't know about the senators and congressmen. Johnson was absolutely ruthless in this pursuit. I have to applaud his ruthlessness because it was in a cause where nobody else could have gotten that law through.

Here would be a typical way he would operate. He would ring up, say, Senator X or Senator Y. But he wouldn't call them in the daytime, afternoon, or early evening. He called them around three a.m. I don't know when Johnson slept, but he would call them at three in the morning and hear this guy come on the phone, and say "This is your president," and the guy would say, "President of what?" Now he is coming awake, and Johnson says, "President of these United States, and I call you up, Senator, because I understand that you are not going to vote for *my* bill." And he [the senator] says, "Lyndon, come on. You are a Southerner. I vote for your bill and they will cut my throat." Johnson says, "You have been in the Congress for thirty-five years, and no one is about to cut your throat, but I will tell you something. If you don't vote for *my* bill, I'll cut your throat."

"Mr. President, that is no way to talk to a U.S. senator." Well, Johnson says, "Let's change the scene a bit. Let's say next

Thursday, front page of the *Washington Post*, the newspaper of record in Washington, DC, and the headlines are about you, Senator, and it says: 'What is the Senator doing in room 346 of the Mayflower Hotel every Saturday night at nine o'clock? Is he up there to say the Our Father with somebody?'" And of course by now the senator is outraged, and he says, "My God, they will kill me." "You got it right. You better vote for *my* bill," and Johnson slammed down the phone.

Well, he literally blackmailed everybody that he had something on, and he had something on just about everybody. And, believe it or not, having dumped that bill in their laps the first week in January, on the first week of July he signed the bill, which had been approved by the majority of senators and congressmen. I swear to you that no president since him could possibly have gotten that bill through Congress, and he got it through because he was ruthless and because he had all the dirt on everybody, and he wasn't above threatening them, and he did it person by person, and he did it when he had them at a disadvantage at three in the morning. The fact is, the message came through: you either go along with the president, or he is going to get you fired from your job. Now that is playing hard-ball, and you don't read much about that in the history books, but that is how that happened. I know because I was there. The bill only got passed because of Lyndon Johnson and [his] being such a tough president.[1]

---

1. The Senate passed the Civil Rights Act of 1964 on June 19 by a vote of 73 to 27. A higher percentage of Republican senators favored the bill than Democratic ones, with 27 voting yea and only 6 nay. On July 2, the House of Representatives approved the bill 289 to 126, with Republicans following the same pattern as in the Senate. The yea votes included 136 Republicans and 152 Democrats—with the nays 35 from the GOP and 91 on the Democratic side. President Johnson signed the bill into law that evening. In *An Idea Whose Time Has Come: Two Presidents, Two Parties, and the Battle for the Civil Rights Act of 1964* (Henry Holt, 2014), Todd S. Purdum reports that Johnson contacted Carl Albert, the House majority leader, shortly after the vote: "Johnson called Albert,

But the fact is that since it was passed, you today don't look on this as a personal obstruction of your liberty. You don't look on it as a bad thing but as a good thing. You look at it as a law that somehow made the words of Jefferson, that all men are created equal and endowed by their Creator with certain unalienable rights, life, liberty and the pursuit of happiness, come true, and the words of Lincoln and the Emancipation Proclamation come true. If you are an American citizen and someone tries to deny you your human rights, [that person] goes to jail—and you go free.

So it was a spectacular moment in history, and history can be pretty dry when you are reading it in a book. But I can tell you from being a part of that history that that was a great day when Lyndon Johnson signed that bill, and from that day on the United States has been true to the ideal that was laid out by the founders of this Republic and by the great Lincoln who upheld it when it was being tried during the great Civil War, which tore the country apart. Today that problem is done, it's buried, it's over, it's finished. So this country today has as good of a law on human rights as any country on earth.

After Lyndon Johnson, Richard Nixon was president, and he appointed you chairman of the Commission on Civil Rights in 1969. You were asked to leave the chairmanship in 1972. Was Nixon involved in that?

---

whose Oklahoma constituents had little fondness for the bill, to congratulate him, adding, 'I guess you know that probably you'll get more congratulations up here than you'll get at home.'" Known by the nickname "the Little Giant from Little Dixie," Albert had opposed civil rights bills in 1956 and 1957. But 1964 proved different, and the diminutive future Speaker of the House wasn't alone in casting a yea vote that constituents back in his district didn't like or support. The presidential arm-twisting and phone-bullying paid off.

No. The Nixon White House began to go sour because of three people: [John] Mitchell, who was attorney general, [John] Ehrlichman, and [H. R.] Haldeman [high-ranking White House staff members]. Those three guys were pretty influential.

I had known him [Nixon] off and on [since the early 1950s], and when he became president I went to see him. I said, "I am the only guy left of the original Civil Rights members, and we pretty much got the basic laws in place, and the problem now is getting people to follow those laws. It's one thing to have a law on the books, and it is another thing to have people administer it and make it a reality." So, I said, "I think it is time that I should get off."

He said, "Let me think about it," so we did some other business that day. I told him that he really ought to give the right to vote to eighteen-year-olds. You see, in those days, when he became president, you couldn't vote unless you were twenty-one. I said, "You've got a very unpopular war, the Vietnam War, and you are getting all these eighteen-year-olds being drafted and going to Vietnam, and thousands of them are getting killed there, and they can't even vote for the commander-in-chief." By golly, he got on it, and we had a constitutional amendment [in 1971].

He came back in a week, and he said, "Father Ted, I would like you to be chairman of the commission." I said, "Mr. President, I say I want to quit because I have been on the job for over a decade. You say you want to put me in charge. It doesn't make any sense." He says, "Well, I think you know this thing pretty well, and I would like to have you in charge." I said, "Well, let me tell you something. There are a few things going on, including in your administration, that are not in keeping with the best of human rights, and I'll be all over you because if I take the job, I am going to do it if I am chairman. I get to lay the agenda." He said, "I want you to be chairman," and I said, "Okay, we'll give it a try, and if it doesn't work, I'll quit."

A year later I decided the federal government was not following its own laws. We had plenty of laws at that time on hiring, on voting, on the administration of justice, and yet the fact is that you could take the greatest departments in Washington, the Department of Justice or the Department of Defense, with thirty thousand to forty thousand people in the department, and when you shake them down, you'd find out the blacks had the lowest possible jobs, and none of the jobs beyond a certain low point. And that wasn't the way the law was written, but they were getting away with it. And so I decided now that I am chairman, we are going to look at the federal government by just assessing the annual reports. They had to report on these things; that was part of our civil rights law. You had to report if you hired a thousand people. You had to report how many were minorities, how many were women, how many were black, et cetera. The commission by that time had a staff of about a hundred and fifty and our own offices in Washington, DC. We took all the big departments that had thirty thousand to forty thousand employees, and we found out that the minorities, especially blacks and Hispanics, were all at the lowest possible levels of employment. All of the juicy jobs up the line were all held by white people.

I always played it straight with the press. I told them the commission is going to take a look at the federal government and how it's obeying its own laws about civil rights. I will have the report ready a year from now [in September 1970], and they are going to have the midterm elections in November of that particular year. Reading all of these reports, our annual assessment of this was devastating. It showed that while we passed laws on the equality in opportunity of hiring so that minority people could come ahead in the world with better-paying jobs, the fact is that ninety-nine percent of them had the lowest jobs in government. The government was the biggest hirer there was in Washington, DC and many other parts of the country, where they had big plants and big departments.

When I got the report finished, I had it printed up and sent a copy over to the White House, to the president, to the vice president, and to every senator and congressman. And the report showed without any doubt that having passed all of these great laws on civil rights, the government itself was not following them at all as far as equality of opportunity to work in the government went, and that was one of the only big ways to lift the minorities up was to give them better jobs if they were qualified—and many of them were by now.

When they read it in the White House, they saw pink, and they called me right away and said, Don't let this out until after the election. The election was coming up, of course, in November. I said, "Look, every reporter in Washington knows I'm doing this report. They all know that I finished the report. They all know that I said publicly when we finish it we are going to publish it, and it was finished last week, and they know that it is going to be published next week."

They [the White House] said, "No, bury it till after the election; this could kill us in the election." I said, "I am not interested in the election. I am more interested in human rights and how they are practiced by this government." So I went ahead and I published it two days later, and I had two hundred people show up at the press conference when we put out the report, and of course the Nixon administration got murdered because it was devastating that in one of the most important parts of civil rights, equal opportunity for jobs, they simply hadn't come through in the federal government.

Whatever jobs there were for minorities were all at the bottom the lowest level.

Well, that of course did not make me very popular with the Nixon administration. Especially with Ehrlichman, Haldeman, and Mitchell, the attorney general. That's when I asked him [Mitchell] to come and testify. He had to show up and testify. He did everything possible to testify badly.

Well, when the Republicans won the election [in 1972, with Nixon being reelected] you can imagine what happened to me. The first thing they did was not to call me. They called my assistant, John Buggs. They said, "Tell your boss that he's fired. He needs to get out of the office by five o'clock tonight. Clear out his desk and get lost." Which is not a very nice thing to say when you have been on the job for fifteen years and changed the face of America through the laws. So John comes into my office, and he is shaking, and I said, "What's up, John?" He said, "I just a got a call from the White House, and boy are they upset. They said to tell you that you are to get out of the office by five o'clock tonight." I said, "John, just calm down, they've got the power to fire the chairman. They appointed the chairman; they could fire the chairman. They couldn't fire me as commissioner, and I still have two years to go as a commissioner." But, I said, "I think it's high time I got out of here, but they are not going to scare me to get out of here by five o'clock tonight. You call back to the White House and tell them I have been here for fifteen years on this job, and it is going to take me a little time to clear out my stuff. I will be out of here by the end of the week. As far as whether I get off the commission, *I* will decide that because the president can't fire me from the commission. He can only fire me as chairman."

So they were all upset and screaming, but I stayed the rest of the week. I had John call them and tell them I was retiring as a member of the commission. That was the end of a fifteen-year experience. I have to say it was quite an education. The press in Washington, luckily, were all on my side. The White House got murdered, and I got wonderful backing from all the press. They said, "How do you feel about it?" I said, "I feel about it like I did when I was appointed. I was appointed fifteen years ago, and I've done the job for fifteen years, and I am retiring with the same spirit with which I took on the job—fired with enthusiasm." I became a national hero by being fired, and it all worked out okay. But those poor guys—Mitchell, Haldeman, and Ehrlichman—all went to federal prison, and I was a free man.

In October of 2007, to celebrate your ninetieth birthday and the displaying of the picture of you and Martin Luther King in the National Portrait Gallery, you also stopped by the White House for a meeting with George W. Bush.

Yes, I went over to see the president and gave him a little advice.

What might that advice have been?

I told him to be relaxed. He is the president of the United States. Nobody can take it away from him. He was elected freely by the people. He knows what he wants to do, and the worst thing he can do is be ground down by the opposition.

I said, "You've got a chance to get some good things done the last year you are in office, so do them. Do them with courage. I'll even give you a motto in Latin, 'Illegitimi non carborundum.'" He said, "What does that mean?" I said, "It's a little brash. It means 'Don't let the bastards grind you down,' which is a free translation [of the aphorism]." So we had a nice visit, and he signed a couple of pictures. He didn't sit behind his desk and pontificate. He came around. He had a couple of chairs in front of his desk facing each other.

I met all of them, and I must say all of the presidents are fundamentally decent people. They get chopped up politically, one way or another. Some are very popular, and some aren't so popular. But, by and large, they have a great responsibility, and, by and large, I found them very decent people. Generally, very good people. That doesn't mean they are going to be sanctified or canonized, because they have their faults too—but, by and large, they are trying to do a tough job, and most of them do it pretty well.

DURING THE CLASS, the name of one former president never came up—Ronald Reagan. What makes this somewhat curious, of course, is that he was more identified with Notre Dame than any other occupant of the White House. The actor-turned-politician had played the school's football hero George Gipp in the popular 1940 film *Knute Rockne, All American*, and Reagan deftly used the nickname of "the Gipper" to rally his political supporters for over two decades. He, in fact, came to the university twice during his presidency: in 1981 to receive an honorary degree and give the commencement address, and in 1988 to dedicate a stamp honoring Rockne. (Think about it: When's the last time a president was involved in a stamp ceremony?)

The 1981 visit received enormous news coverage. It was the first trip outside Washington for Reagan after he was shot and seriously injured in an assassination attempt two months earlier. Sharing the stage with the president that day was the actor Pat O'Brien, who portrayed Rockne in the movie and was also an honorary degree recipient.

Saluting Reagan, Father Hesburgh took a serious approach and then a more amusing as well as parochial one: "We welcome the president of the United States back to health. We welcome the president of the United States back into the body of his people, the Americans, and lastly, here at Notre Dame, here in a very special way, we welcome the Gipper at long last back to get his degree." The applause was thunderous.

Despite the tie to the university, the two men, just six years apart in age, were never personally close. In a subsequent conversation in his office after the former president died, Father Hesburgh confided that Reagan always seemed distant and difficult to get to know. Smiling pleasantries and sociable small talk came naturally to the Gipper, but the priest and U.S. president never went into deeper waters of policy or world affairs. Maybe the closeness of Father Hesburgh to Jimmy Carter, whom Reagan defeated in 1980, had something to do with it. Maybe it was more deeply rooted. The pair had publicly clashed over the treatment of student protesters in the late 1960s, when Reagan was governor of California and known for maintaining a hardline approach in dealing with campuses there. In any case, it was a cordial yet remote relationship.

Interestingly, that didn't stop Father Hesburgh from trying to reduce their distance. He made one other presentation to Reagan before leaving the Notre Dame presidency. On October 24, 1982, he went to the White House for a special event in part orchestrated by the university. Here's the entry in *The Reagan Diaries* (2007) about the evening:

Having a dinner with sports flavor. Father Hesburgh of N.D. is presenting us with a print of "Knute Rockne, All American." I've never owned one. So dinner with lots of sports figures & a running of the film.

It was quite an experience to see it again after all these years and to see it in such company—Sonny Jorgenson [*sic*], Gale Sayers, Merlin Olson [*sic*], Joe Theisman [*sic*]—the Notre Dame Coach [Gerry Faust], and many, many more. For me it was a truly nostalgic evening.

Reagan's rendering, complete with misspelled or missing names, puts the emphasis on viewing his most notable cinematic role again and the company of athletic personalities who attended. The person responsible for providing the entertainment receives a mention—but nothing more.

At the end of the class, Father Hesburgh pulled me aside in the backstage area of the auditorium. In a concerned voice, he wanted to know how he had handled himself in front of the students and television cameras. After I assured him that the session couldn't have gone better from my perspective, he said, "If you think I'm having trouble speaking in front of people, let me know. I don't want to do anything in public if I'm not at my best. I trust you to tell me."

He understood he was getting older and worried about making an impression different from what he had in the past. A man in the public eye for so long was sensitive to how he might be perceived by a new generation of students.

Father Hesburgh took special pride in his collection of books autographed by their authors, which he presented to the library on campus for special care and safekeeping. Included among the nearly two thousand volumes are several by former presidents. Congenitally inquisitive (some might just say nosy), I was curious which president sent the most signed copies. Would it be Dwight Eisenhower? Or Jimmy Carter? Possibly Bill Clinton?

Believe it or not, it was Richard Nixon, but what's fascinating is that after the Watergate revelations and his resignation from office in 1974, he provided only his signature on the books he sent to Father Hesburgh. In his 1992 book *Seize the Moment*, he affixed a formal autograph—"Richard Nixon"—for Father Hesburgh, yet for Father Joyce he wrote a more personal inscription:

> To Father Edmund Joyce—
> With many pleasant
> memories of our friendship
> over the years.
> From
> Dick Nixon
> 3-3-'92

Interestingly, Nixon didn't send Father Hesburgh a copy of *Leaders* (1982). However, Father Joyce did receive the book, with this handwritten tribute:

> To Reverend Edmund Joyce—
> With appreciation for his
> service to the cause of
> academic & athletic excellence—
> From his friend
> Richard Nixon
> 12-7-82

Like most presidents, Nixon was a complicated public figure, even to his selection of book recipients and how he would handle each volume. He might have been behind the firing of Father Hesburgh from the chairmanship of the Commission on Civil Rights, but the former president kept in touch in his way. When we were talking one day over cigars in his office, Father Hesburgh recalled that he had been at a formal dinner in New York a decade or so after Nixon's resignation. Also on the dais was former president Gerald Ford. When the priest got up to talk, he followed what he considered the appropriate protocol by acknowledging the twice-elected Nixon first and the never-elected Ford second. Every other speaker had done the reverse, Ford first with Nixon second. From that point until Nixon's death in 1994, the two men exchanged messages of one kind or another. One considerate gesture opened the door.

After Barack Obama won the 2008 presidential election, he came to Notre Dame on May 17, 2009, to receive an honorary degree and to speak at the commencement ceremony. His stands on abortion and other subjects made his visit, in a word, controversial. Prior to his arrival, a small plane flew over the campus, dragging a large sign featuring a gruesome picture of an aborted fetus on it.

Writing about these protests in the *South Bend Tribune* after Father Hesburgh died, columnist Jack Colwell recalled speaking with the priest in a local restaurant at the time. "I'd like to go up and shoot down that damn plane," Colwell remembered Father Hesburgh saying, with a smile that signaled he was being facetious. "But I suppose that would not be appropriate."

Father Hesburgh's commitment to pro-life causes was well-known, but in Obama's case other factors assumed significance and deserved consideration. As the first African American president, he was fulfilling a dream of the U.S. Commission on Civil Rights and of the legislation Lyndon Johnson fought for and signed into law during 1964 and 1965. Indeed, when Obama met Father Hesburgh for the first time, he credited the priest's civil rights work as instrumental in opening the doors of the White House to a person from a minority, such as himself.

A narrow, single-issue approach wasn't Father Hesburgh's style. He took a more comprehensive view, respecting the presidency as a national—rather than as a partisan political—institution. His approach angered some Notre Dame alumni and American Catholics, but he maintained a constancy about the centrality of the White House as a place where resolute leadership, domestically and internationally, was a daily imperative.

The author and Father Hesburgh after a dinner in 2006 recognizing the twentieth anniversary of the Hesburgh Lecture Series, which the Notre Dame Alumni Association sponsors. Faculty from across the university participate in the program, which provides speakers from campus to alumni clubs and communities throughout the country. Photo courtesy of Joe Raymond.

Lessons from Friendship

Starting in the late 1990s, Father Hesburgh took a professional—at times even paternal—interest in a journalism program for undergraduates. On January 18, 1996, he wrote an introductory letter to a friend, the president of the John S. and James L. Knight Foundation, requesting initial funding to launch a novel approach for preparing students for careers in different aspects of news. That letter opens on a personal note: "While I am in retirement here, I am constantly visited by students with a wide variety of problems and professors who are seeking my interest and support in their projects. Really, it is like being everybody's grandfather. I like it."

Father Hesburgh's letter and a follow-up proposal I drafted did the trick, creating the Notre Dame Program for Journalism, Ethics and Democracy. Even before the Knight Foundation's seed money was spent, the family of John W. Gallivan endowed the program in perpetuity. Both Father Hesburgh and Father Joyce were friends of Jack Gallivan, class of 1937 (the same year as Father Joyce) and the retired publisher of the *Salt Lake Tribune*. The priests, in fact, visited the Gallivans in

Utah during their cross-country, recreational-vehicle adventure after retiring.

Without fail, when Father Hesburgh received invitations to Gallivan Program activities, he participated. He also enjoyed journalists' visits to campus for lectures or classroom sessions, and they reported behind-the-scenes information to him. At those meetings he had a chance to discuss events in his own past in connection to contemporary affairs. He still knew most of the players and how the games were played.

Outside of these occasions, we met with some regularity in his office on the thirteenth floor of the Hesburgh Library to talk about matters either close to home or far away. And, from time to time, my phone would ring and Melanie Chapleau, who singlehandedly managed Father Hesburgh's appointments, messages, and most everything else, would say, "Can you come over and talk to Father?" Whatever I was doing at the moment could wait.

During one of our last conversations—he was sitting in a comfortable chair placed just behind his desk, perfuming his office with a sizable stogie—I reminded him of one of our visits to the Grotto on campus and mentioned I might compose a short article about it. He smiled broadly, as much as to say, "Be my guest."

I sent the reminiscence to *Notre Dame Magazine* early in January 2015. Written throughout in the present tense, the essay was intended to capture a humorous, yet touching scene for old times' sake. Sadly, when Father Hesburgh passed away six weeks later, I had to change all of the verbs to the past tense.

That story—revised from the version published in the spring 2015 issue—follows, along with others that I jotted down in a notebook over the years. These vignettes (I hope) provide a glimpse of a public figure away from the spotlight and the hurly-burly of a varied life—someone who remained fascinating for what he said and how he said it until his last days.

WHENEVER IT WAS POSSIBLE, Father Theodore Hesburgh, C.S.C., liked to make a short stop on Holy Cross Drive near Saint Mary's Lake if he was traveling around the Notre Dame campus.

"Would you mind pulling over to the side here?" he usually inquired—and nobody ever minded. Even with diminished eyesight caused by macular degeneration, he knew right where he was from the curves in the road and the familiar surroundings.

Not far off to the side there is the Grotto of Our Lady of Lourdes, where he had prayed since he first arrived at Notre Dame as a student in 1934.

The ritual of the brief sojourn rarely varied. There was the saying of a Hail Mary or two and the occasional special blessing for the driver and other passengers in the car.

A couple years ago, though, the routine took an amusing turn. With prayers offered and amens pronounced, Father Hesburgh looked at the Grotto's glow cast against the night's darkness and quipped in deadpan fashion, "I should have asked for the candle concession."

"You could have retired to some exotic island by now," he was informed in a jesting reply.

Never to be outdone, the priest—no stranger to conversing with presidents and popes as well as people of all ranks and religions—retorted matter-of-factly, "I'd own the island by now."

While the Main Building (crowned with its nineteen-foot statue of Mary) and the Hesburgh Library (featuring the multistory mosaic of Jesus with raised arms) are imposing to anyone seeing them for the first—or for the hundredth—time, the Grotto is unique. Lacking the formality of the Basilica of the Sacred Heart, nestled among trees in the back of campus, the setting and its statue are both public and intimate at the same time.

This shrine was originally proposed by Notre Dame's founder, Rev. Edward Sorin, C.S.C., and built in 1896, three years after his death. Since then, the Grotto and what it signifies have possessed something akin to a magnetic attraction for students, alumni, and others.

Perhaps it's a quick prayer for a family member, or the lighting of a candle for a problem that just doesn't seem to resolve itself, or even a rosary for someone recently departed. The Grotto for many people, including Father Hesburgh (fittingly called the university's second founder for his long and eventful tenure as president), was—and will always be—a singular place.

For someone like me, who's crossed the Rubicon of senior citizenship (that milestone year of sixty-five) and confronted intimations of mortality recuperating from two cardiac repair jobs (complete both times with incarceration in intensive care units), priorities shift and somersault. It's as though there's a new angle of vision on day-to-day activities, a prism providing new perspective.

Today it's become second nature for me to detour by the shrine while walking on campus near the Main Building or to slow my car to a crawl while driving near the Grotto.

Out of doors (*en plein air*, as the French say), this Notre Dame landmark quietly emphasizes the Marian devotion and mystique that have animated this sacred precinct since 1842. It's that, of course, but really much more, too.

Any jocular aspirations of acquiring the candle concession were—and should have been—the province of another and much more worthy claimant. Someone who kept the university's namesake at the center of his life for over eight decades. The rest of us will be content to make time to stop at the Grotto, if only for a few minutes, either by serendipity or chance—or for a definite reason.

There, for well over a century while the university has developed so dramatically, men and women have come with earthly intentions in need of celestial attention. There, too, these men and women have found reassuring solace in the abiding and beckoning light—as Father Hesburgh always did.

As I GOT TO KNOW Father Hesburgh better, I found his humor and wit both sly and wry. In a conversation, he could put you at ease by referring to himself, as mentioned earlier, as "an old goat" while occasionally worrying out loud about "losing my marbles." During our last extended session before he died, I asked whether he looked forward to an exhibit of his awards, photographs, and mementos that was planned as part of the renovation of the Hesburgh Library. "I'd put everything in one room and lock the door," he responded. In the same discussion, he asked about a book I was finishing. "That will be your twelfth, right?" he wondered. How his "marbles" remembered the correct number I'll never know.

Quips and gentle mockery came from his lips more easily the more time you spent with him. Before a campus dinner at which I had asked him to say grace, I went to his office—it was a Sunday evening—to pick him up. A graduate student was reading a new book about Islam to him when I arrived. Without a pause I was informed, "You're early. Sit down. You might learn something."

Another time I saw Father Hesburgh having some trouble getting out of a campus security car that had delivered him to the library. When he was safely out of his seat and on terra firma, he turned back and offered the officer an elaborate blessing that covered the man, his family, and all future progeny to whom he might be related.

When the door was closed and the vehicle moving away, I inquired about the parting ritual. Before taking a step, Father Hesburgh shrugged and said matter-of-factly, "You've got to give him something." (I later learned that the security officer was himself a part-time minister who much appreciated being on the receiving end of prayer.)

When we were talking about what was happening on campus, he'd often take up his linguistic scalpel and make a small incision or two on people at Notre Dame. One time, when I was involved in a vexing situation that's not worth explaining, the man dedicated to the peaceful resolution of conflicts offered a rather direct approach to correct the problem with the culprit responsible: "I'd take out a shotgun and settle things that way."

He complained that "with the Puritans in the Main Building you can't smoke anywhere on campus." His mischievous will, however, always found a way to pursue his habitual puffing. He considered it something of an entitlement in his Hesburgh Library office. When I asked him whether it was true that he personally maneuvered to add a smoking room to Holy Cross House—the retirement center for priests to which he moved a decade before his death—he confessed, "I got it paid for," and then added an even more revealing comment: "I don't ever assume there are any secrets around here." Two decades removed from serving as president, he understood that people still talked about him and that gossip traveled quickly in a small community.

A certain earthy vernacular occasionally entered his speech, making what he was saying more vivid. He called the classes he conducted as a guest lecturer "one-night stands." In his office, he'd excuse himself to use the plumbing, saying, "Sorry. I've got old man's disease."

On September 12, 2002, we were seated across from each other at a university dinner. It was one year after the terrorist attacks of 9/11, and Bill Clinton had impressively held forth the previous night on the *Late Show with David Letterman*. Noting that the discussion reflected a mastery of subjects on the part of the former president, I mentioned Clinton's brain power. To the astonishment of the six other people at the table, the priest (who had received the Congressional Gold Medal from Clinton two years before) said, "Bob, his problem isn't his brains. It's his gonads."

As Father Hesburgh's macular degeneration got progressively worse, diminishing what remained of his eyesight, he'd solicit advice on what to say for an upcoming speech on campus—and then lament his inability to use any notes or an outline. During an interview a decade before he died, he told me, "I can't write anything. I can't read anything. It's all got to come out of your bean." Bean? Yes. Interestingly, when he stood at a podium, it often appeared that he was looking down to consult a document, but that, I think, was force of habit—and an attempt to mask the sad reality.

Sometimes his eye problems produced unintentional humor, particularly for other people. In late 2001, Katie and Daire Keogh, friends from Dublin, stopped by Katie's alma mater with their newborn son, John, who was being transported in a baby carrier. Along with two friends, Father Hesburgh entered the restaurant where we were eating, and Daire, an Irish historian of note, asked me to invite him over to the table to bless little John. Uneasy at interrupting someone during a social occasion, I tried to dodge the request—but to no avail.

When I approached Father Hesburgh, he acted as though it wouldn't be the slightest inconvenience, and he came to our table. After exchanging greetings and talking about his own Irish heritage—his mother's maiden name was Murphy—Father Hesburgh wanted to fulfill his priestly duty. There, however, was one problem. He raised it straightforwardly with a question: "Where's the baby?" The parents pointed to the carrier on the floor, and the priest set to work.

On July 30, 2013—as it happened, my sixty-fifth birthday—I had a follow-up appointment with the cardiac surgeon who had performed a quadruple bypass on me five weeks earlier. Getting ready to leave the hospital complex, my wife and I ran into Father Hesburgh and Melanie Chapleau, who was navigating his wheelchair. He was there for an X-ray.

We all started talking, and two or three times Father Hesburgh interjected, "You're looking good, Bob." Of course, he was trying to be encouraging after the recent ordeal—including nearly two weeks in intensive care and the excruciating pain from a simple sneeze or cough—but it still seemed oddly amusing to hear the upbeat visual assessment from someone without much ability to see. We parted company when a hospital orderly inquired for all to hear, "Is there a Theodore here?"

DESPITE THE PERSISTENT PROBLEMS with his eyesight, Father Hesburgh worked diligently to stay connected to and, as much as possible, involved in the concerns that had animated his earlier years. Matters of the Church, education, peace, civil rights, and world affairs continued to occupy his thinking and discussions. When travel to board meetings or firsthand inspections of a foreign situation became too difficult for him to undertake alone, student readers helped provide a bridge to the outer world. They came to his office daily, following a preplanned schedule. He often commented on whatever subjects the students were reading about, so there was a fair exchange of information.

Besides the succession of readers, he constantly listened to television news reports throughout the day and always kept a book on tape nearby. In May 2011 Father Hesburgh had kidney surgery, and he was recuperating in Holy Cross House. I stopped by to say hello and to see how he was doing—but had trouble trying to start a conversation. Fox News was at full volume on his TV in his sitting area *and* the machine playing a recorded book was at a similar sound level right next to him.

Remarking that it was next to impossible to talk, I picked up the television remote and clicked it off. "You didn't have to do that," he said unhappily—so I turned it back on at a decreased volume. On his own, he stopped the machine reading the book.

After catching up and telling him I was taking off the next day for a lecture in Vienna followed by teaching of a summer class in Notre Dame's Dublin program, I thought it might be appropriate to take my leave, saying, "You probably want to take a nap." That prompted the response "I never take naps" and a suggestion that the two of us listen to a book about Winston Churchill's decision making during World War II. I expected to listen for five or ten minutes of the tape (along with his color commentary) but, alas, couldn't stage a retreat until the chapter was finished—more than a half hour later.

Walking out of Holy Cross House, it dawned on me that Father Hesburgh's considerable regard for Churchill might have resulted from the priest's own self-image as well as his admiration from afar. Of course, both men loved their large cigars, recognized that leadership involves the marriage of a definite vision and inspiring oratory, and were involved in a host of problems during their long lives. Then I thought back to the time, a few years earlier, when Father Hesburgh began to use a walking stick. He had told me when he got it, "Churchill said that you *wear* a cane." The two figures—each able to compose and dictate letters and statements with rapidity and originality—shared more than a few superficial traits, though Churchill, to be sure, was on a plane all his own. But some parallels certainly existed for idle, pointy-headed speculation.

During one of our interviews, Father Hesburgh referred to himself as "a nut on correspondence," and the truth of that description was never in doubt. The U.S. Postal Service and Notre Dame's internal campus mail system delivered thousands of his dictated epistles and handwritten notes over the years. If a letter asked a question, you could expect a quick answer, unless he was traveling. Shortly after the Christmas and New Year's vacation one year, I stopped by his office and saw three boxes of cards and other greetings that had recently arrived. He always kept in touch with his far-flung network of friends and acquaintances.

Some notes that he dictated and sent to me provided interesting background to better understand an event or activity more completely. In the summer of 2000, just before Father Hesburgh received the Congressional Gold Medal in the Capitol rotunda, a White House speechwriter called for a little guidance on the remarks he was composing for Bill Clinton. As more of a favor for the medal's recipient than the medal presenter, I suggested some revisions and new lines—and then headed to Washington a few days later for the actual ceremony.

Preoccupied with peace talks between the Israelis and the Palestinians taking place outside Washington, Clinton helicoptered to the Capitol at the last moment and spoke extemporaneously rather than using the text that had been written for him. I wondered why, and, heading to the reception Notre Dame sponsored after the event, it occurred to me that one of life's most frustrating jobs must be to write speeches for other people that go undelivered.

But, happily, the story doesn't end with words not spoken. Three months later (October 24, to be precise), Senator Joseph Lieberman, the Democratic vice-presidential candidate that year, came to Notre Dame for an address on faith and values in Washington Hall. Sitting in the media section (two decades of political analysis on local television took me to many such speeches), I listened more intently as Lieberman began telling an anecdote about Father Hesburgh. The story was originally part of Clinton's Gold Medal remarks, and the part I had a hand in crafting. I surmised that the speechwriter (who also wrote for Al Gore) had left the administration as the presidential campaign took center stage and was doing some authorial recycling in the fall.

I sent Father Hesburgh a note and Lieberman's address, explaining what had happened. Grateful to know what was said about him, he responded, "At the Congressional Gold Medal Ceremony, President Clinton skipped the greater part of the talk prepared for him and spoke from his heart which I thought he did very well." Someone must have sent the honoree the text or told him about it, so he knew that "the greater part of the talk" wasn't delivered.

Despite all of Clinton's personal problems, Father Hesburgh rarely expressed an ill word about him, the little jab about "gonads" notwithstanding. After a speaking trip to Little

Rock and a day of rubbernecking at the William J. Clinton Presidential Center and Park in 2006, I sent Father Hesburgh a note that he was mentioned in one of the exhibits on display. In response, he said, "I didn't know I was in the Clinton Library but happy that I am because he was a good President, I think, and I am not afraid to be associated with him." In the priest's view, presidents of whatever party deserved (in the phrase included near the beginning of the Declaration of Independence) "a decent respect." That opinion extended to Clinton, who had been impeached, and to Richard Nixon, who had been forced to resign in disgrace. From up-close observation and governmental service, the priest understood better than most people the burdens of the nation's highest office.

Until his macular degeneration stopped him from reading anything, Father Hesburgh (who seemed to be on almost every organization's mailing list) would forward to me any reports, journals, or newsletters he received that focused on the news media or politics. Often these publications arrived with a small, preprinted form from the president emeritus with a menu of options:

for your information
for your files
for appropriate action
please prepare reply for my signature
please answer direct
please send copy of reply
please advise me
please read and return

Near the bottom of the form was space for him to jot "Remarks." One that arrived in late December 1997 read simply,

"Merry Xmas. Fr. Ted." The "Xmas" (rather than "Christmas") struck an old altar server as oddly secular, but it was the shorthand style of a busy person still determined to remain in touch on substantive matters. Other notes said nothing more than "All the best to you. Fr. Ted."

Father Hesburgh took pride in *not* having a cell phone, computer, tablet, or any other communication device of the modern age. For him a landline telephone and a dictating machine were sufficient tools. In contemporary parlance, he wouldn't qualify as a multitasker. Yet, from another perspective, he was the consummate multitasker, able to juggle myriad responsibilities at the same time without slighting the work involved in each.

In 2014 I asked him whether (as Notre Dame's president) he kept in touch with people on campus while he was engaged in Washington meetings or traveling throughout the world. "When I was gone, I was gone," he answered, and then talked about Father Joyce, as executive vice president, being the "inside" decision maker for much of university's pressing business when the president was elsewhere. The Hesburgh–Joyce team operated together for thirty-five years, and Father Hesburgh often said that Father Joyce's death in 2004 was comparable to losing a close family member.

How did this old-style multitasker accomplish so much in so many different arenas for so long? He accepted (in a word he often used) "jobs" that brought his moral orientation and expertise to an issue or problem. He then dictated his schedule for being away from Notre Dame. Like any faithful priest, he went where he was needed, or called, at a particular time. If there happened to be conflicting commitments, he participated in the meetings or activities that had, in his judgment, the potential for the most significant impact on the matter at hand.

During better than a quarter century as president emeritus, Father Hesburgh maintained a schedule that most people between the ages of seventy and ninety-seven would have found daunting. Even after he put a halt to frequent travel, invitations to offer Mass in dorms, speak in classes, and participate in university events arrived on an almost daily basis. He rarely declined.

In the 1990s and the first years of the twenty-first century, Father Hesburgh (in a manner of speaking) evolved. Students, alumni, and others called him, with increasing frequency, simply "Father Ted." The sobriquet married the priestly vocation that had defined him since his ordination in 1943 to a distance-reducing, diminutive form of his first name. He was, as he liked to say, "everybody's grandfather," and that role kept him both busy and involved, especially in dealing with undergraduates.

In September 2012, the student magazine *Scholastic* published an unforgettable picture of Father Hesburgh smoking a cigar with some twenty students from Zahm Hall, celebrating Father Hesburgh's ninety-fifth birthday and the hall's seventy-fifth anniversary. The young men shown—all wearing ties and most attired in suits or sport coats—seem to regard this dorm activity as an initiation rite. Many hold their cigars uncertainly, most likely with first-time awkwardness. Just one youth is smiling. The veteran smoker, seated in the middle of the photograph, looks natural as he holds forth. Unlike the others, he's at ease, with his clerical collar removed and his cigar cradled at the appropriate angle.

After his death in 2015, students and others regularly left cigars on his simple headstone in the cemetery for Holy Cross priests and brothers near Moreau Seminary. Among other things, Father Ted was being remembered for his longstanding habit, with its faint aroma of going against the grain of the time's smokeless aspirations. At one point while I was working on the first draft of this book, I planned to call it *Cigars with Father Ted*. Cooler, more sensitive heads prevailed. But the priest was in a league with Churchill and Mark Twain in his attachment to this venial vice.

As much as he got around to attend this or that function on campus, his roomy office on the thirteenth floor of the Hesburgh Library was the place most associated with his twilight years. Correspondence originated there, and visitors—with or without appointments—stopped by. Mass was frequently offered in the chapel next to a larger meeting room, and his desk (where he heard countless student confessions) was positioned to take advantage of a window facing west. From it you can see much of the campus, with the Main Building and Sacred Heart Basilica dominating the view. Even with his restricted vision, he still tried to focus on the statue of Mary atop the dome. He frequently looked up from his desk for a quick prayer to her or to seek her help with something. Very few people left 1315 Hesburgh Library without hearing how much the golden likeness of Our Lady outside his window meant to him.

One of his last outings from Holy Cross House, as he declined, was a farewell visit to his office, which was always much more than a place for a retiree to pass time. Indeed, throughout almost all his years after leaving the presidency, he spent several hours, *seven* days a week there to keep up with everything and to stay connected with people near and far. Surrounded by shelves of books, awards, pictures with presidents and popes, and other memorabilia, someone could easily understand why the occupant would want this suite of rooms as his principal sanctum.

Just making his way to the thirteenth floor of the library kept him connected to the lives of students. They all recognized him as he approached the elevator. Invariably, he asked them questions (about classes, teachers, dorm life, whatever), and students later talked among themselves about the fortuitous encounters.

Anyone who met or knew Father Hesburgh quickly realized how much he enjoyed talking, and he conversed easily with world leaders, the less fortunate in developing countries, and every stratum of humankind in between. He was also a talented storyteller. As noted earlier, certain accounts describing his own experiences and exploits came up with such frequency that they approached the category of greatest hits. For someone who brought journalists by to meet Father Hesburgh, it was astonishing to listen to favorite tales repeated exactly as they were told before. He never tired of relating his experiences on the U.S. Commission on Civil Rights or the International Atomic Energy Agency.

Many times, though, he'd bring up something that happened in the past, and a listener wanted to learn more. During one saunter down memory lane, we were talking about his efforts to improve the faculty and I brought up the name of Rev. John A. O'Brien, whom I remembered from student days for the simple reason that he worked and *lived* in the Main Building, which struck me as out of the ordinary, if not strange. I knew he was a well-known popular writer on religious matters, but I was curious why Notre Dame had several endowed professorships named for this particular priest.

It was simple, Father Hesburgh explained. He remembered a knock on his office door in the Main Building one evening, and Father O'Brien entered in a glum mood.

"I've got a problem," announced the unhappy cleric, a diocesan priest from Illinois and a member of the Notre Dame faculty since 1940. His problem? The books, pamphlets, and articles he wrote produced considerable income, and he didn't know how to handle it all.

Father Hesburgh described Father O'Brien as frugal to the point of desperately needing to purchase a new cassock and to buy a car newer and more reliable than the one he'd driven for many years. Be that as it may, Notre Dame's president promised to help Father O'Brien in his plight.

After his death in 1980, Father O'Brien left an estate worth several million dollars to the university. In a letter, before announcing the gift in 1981, Father Hesburgh wrote, "John O'Brien wanted this legacy to be an endowment and pretty much left it to me to decide to what purposes the endowment might best be directed." At the time, the university was directing a high percentage of new resources to creating endowed academic chairs to attract and keep noted scholar-teachers. Today the interest from the original benefaction funds a dozen professorships at Notre Dame, a fellowship program for doctoral students in the Catholic intellectual tradition, and a library collection in theology and philosophy.

Father O'Brien's "problem" ultimately became a notable source of support for academic advancement during the Hesburgh years and afterwards. Royalties from such works as *The Faith of Millions*—published in twenty-eight editions and translated into ten languages—provided a foundation for the future. In talking about Father O'Brien, Father Hesburgh also mentioned another fact I didn't know: John A. O'Brien was the first priest ever to receive the Laetare Medal, Notre Dame's most prestigious award for an American Catholic for service to the Church and wider society. He received the medal in 1973 and later became one of the very few non–Holy Cross clerics to be buried in Holy Cross Cemetery.

As proud as Father Hesburgh seemed to be of the scholarly progress across the different colleges that took place after 1952, late-in-life conversations offered balanced appraisals of the benefits of building centers of excellence and what he perceived as potential negative consequences of Notre Dame's strides forward and institutional changes. He worried about how best to maintain a high percentage of Catholics on the faculty, and he grumbled that some young professors sought hefty salaries without spending very much time in the classroom. He continued to care, but religiously avoided intervening in day-to-day affairs unless asked for an opinion or for assistance in opening a door.

In the last chapter of his autobiography, *God, Country, Notre Dame* (1990), Father Hesburgh wrote that he and Father Joyce "both believed that the best gift we could give to the new administrative team [led by incoming president, Rev. Edward A. Malloy, C.S.C.] was to disappear for a year, and then to slip back quietly and undertake some unobtrusive, nonadministrative tasks that might be useful to the university." The two priests kept their word, and Father Hesburgh often said he no longer made decisions for Notre Dame, just choices of where he'd devote his own time and attention. He was, in his phrase, "a utility outfielder" who responded to the manager's call when he was needed—but not otherwise.

BY WATCHING WHAT HE DID and listening to what he said over decades, I learned as much from Father Hesburgh as anyone else I've known. He was a large figure of vast, worldly experience that he liked to explain, if not relive, but he would also do or say small things that proved instructive. Sometimes he'd stop midsentence or out of earshot of others to offer a lesson.

In 2010—by then he held onto the shoulder of the person with him for guidance and support—we were going into the

Morris Inn for a dinner of the Gallivan Program. A well-known couple, generous benefactors of Notre Dame, was coming toward us, and I whispered their names over my shoulder. After hellos were exchanged, Father Hesburgh began a brief discourse he must have recited hundreds, possibly thousands, of times. He looked directly at the woman and man, who had funded an institute and a building on campus, and told them how much they had strengthened the university with their gifts. The little theme of the message—"we couldn't do anything without people like you"—was not only sincere but also warm.

As they departed, Father Hesburgh had something to say to me that they wouldn't hear. "Bob, remember this: You can't say thank you enough. Don't ever stop saying thank you." He understood that the expression of gratitude was important in itself as well as being a down payment on future generosity.

When we dropped off our coats in the Morris Inn's check room, Father Hesburgh performed a ritual I'd seen many times over the years. He reached into his pocket and extracted a small comb. People would recognize him, he knew, and looking right for a public occasion was part of head-turning recognition, even at the age of ninety-three.

That night, as I helped him out of the car and walked him to the entrance of Holy Cross House, he seemed to have more energy than earlier in the evening. After we shook hands, he made a point of having the last word. "When you need me, you just have to call." He still enjoyed a social occasion with students, journalists, and benefactors.

Beyond his personal imperative of offering daily Mass, praying at other times throughout the day was second nature to Father Hesburgh. Stops at the Grotto were frequent—by foot before walking became difficult and later by car, as described earlier in this chapter. The request for a blessing was never an imposition, just part of being who he was.

Before chauffeuring him to a student dinner one evening, I stopped by his office as he was starting to say the rosary. (When it became impossible for him to read the breviary, he received permission to recite three rosaries each day as a replacement ritualistic practice.) He asked me to join him, and, at the end, he commented that taking time to pray was fine, but that *making* time to pray throughout the day was even better. Rather than being the devil's workshop, idle moments are ideal times for short prayers, regardless of where you are. More than anything, he was suggesting that matins or vespers aren't the only moments to stop and say a prayer. As he told visitors and groups with regularity, the simplest of prayers to deal with challenges was often on his lips: "Come, Holy Spirit." That he recited the rosary just before he died and had also offered Mass earlier that day puts his own prayer life in a more personal perspective.

Father Hesburgh dreamed large dreams for Notre Dame and the wider world, but he was always a realist. As birthdays came and went, with the passing years approaching a full century, he dealt with aging's aches and pains, frustrations and limitations as straightforwardly (and stoically) as possible. Wry lines about hopes or difficulties became part of his repertoire for conversation, but, down deeper, he knew he had to play the cards that were dealt to him.

As I'll explain in the next chapter, his informal yet oft-stated philosophy for dealing with the vagaries of senior citizenship boiled down to one sentence: "Do as much as you can, as well as you can, as long as you can, and don't complain about the things you can no longer do."

Five years after he said this to me, I mentioned to him that I was thinking of retiring at age sixty-five to concentrate on a long-term book project in need of completion. The exchange that followed went just like this:

> **TMH:** "You can't."
> **RS:** "Why?"
> **TMH:** "You should go to seventy. That's what I did. Deal?"
> **RS:** "I've got to get this book finished, and I either need a year's leave or to retire to do that."
> **TMH:** "Take a leave and come back when the book's done. Deal?"
> **RS:** "Well, I don't know."
> **TMH:** "Deal?"
> **RS:** "Okay—if I get the leave."
> **TMH:** "Good. We've got a deal."

I received the leave, completed the book, and now plan to retire—God willing—the month I turn seventy years old. After that I look forward to writing as much as I can, as well as I can, as long as I can. That's become the deal with myself.

In 2010, when Father Hesburgh was ninety-three, we were visiting in his office. He was fidgeting in his chair and had a somewhat troubled look on his face. "Can I get you anything?" I asked.

"Can you make me twenty years younger?" he replied.

The quip is revealing. It concedes that getting older presents its challenges, but it also conveys his desire to turn back the clock so he can keep going. In a way, it says, "Ah, to be seventy-three again," with two more decades of retirement ahead. A certain satisfaction with life comes across in his question as well. In 1990, *God, Country, Notre Dame* appeared and became a national bestseller, and he was able to juggle several off-campus responsibilities as well as travel constantly. New doors opened without the worry of day-to-day administration, and he was happy to walk through them.

As his ability to see diminished, however, he was forced to reduce and ultimately bring an end to assignments away from Notre Dame. In the later years, when I saw his work in civil rights or some other area mentioned in a book or article, I made a point of stopping by to tell him about it. In effect, I became one of his readers, though on an irregular basis—but I drew the line in one respect.

After I published a collection of essays, I sent him a copy with a thank-you for providing several reports that I used in writing the magazine and newspaper pieces now between hard covers. His letter of acknowledgement included this sentence: "If there are specific parts of it [the book] that you think I should read, I would be very happy to have you stop by and read them which could also lead to a discussion of sorts between us."

It was a flattering invitation. Essayists by nature are deluded by ego and vanity, but this request was too much. I couldn't, and didn't, do it. In one of our long interviews, I asked Father Hesburgh about the notable men and women he'd met over the years. He mentioned presidents of countries, popes, cardinals, and astronauts, concluding with a general observation: "You cease to be awed."

Other people are different. In 2006, a few months before Father Hesburgh dictated that note to me, Harper Lee, the author of the novel *To Kill a Mockingbird*, received an honorary degree from Notre Dame. These two household names with much in common met, and she autographed a copy of her classic with this austere yet powerful inscription in her distinctive hand: "To Father Hesburgh in awe."

I shared that feeling, even as I got to know him better and we talked, more informally, about the past and contemporary affairs. A small dictionary I've consulted for years defines *awe* as "reverential fear or wonder." No fear ever intruded on our friendship, but I never overcame the wonder.

Throughout his retirement years, Father Hesburgh always welcomed occasions with students, whether spiritual, instructional, or social. This initiation rite in cigar smoking took place in September 2012 and celebrated Father Hesburgh's ninety-fifth birthday as well as Zahm Hall's seventy-fifth anniversary. Photo courtesy of Joe Raymond.

FIVE

An Unretiring Retirement

The staff of *Notre Dame Magazine*, especially its editor, Kerry Temple, began preparing a commemorative special issue about Father Hesburgh's life and work more than a decade before his death. The plan from the start was that the issue would be published a couple of months after he passed away.

As one of the invited contributors, I was asked to spend time with Father Hesburgh to learn about and then recount what he was doing and thinking during the years after he served as Notre Dame's president. What were his retirement days like? Was he continuing to travel with his purposeful wanderlust? Why did certain concerns rather than others concentrate his attention after the age of seventy?

Writers usually like to complete assignments and then move on to the next wrestling match with the mother tongue. This journalistic exercise, however, proved far different. I submitted the original copy in 2005—and then, at the editor's urging, promised to keep watching the story's subject to insert updates or changes when they seemed necessary. The extra decade of work that followed required reading any and all news accounts as they appeared and posing questions, from time to time, directly to Father Hesburgh. To say that the continuing process of refining that article played a role in composing this book would be a large understatement.

For this chapter, I rely on the reporting for the commemorative profile (titled "The Long Twilight") and additional research that I thought might take the reader closer to the central figure of this volume. My hope is that the amendments and amplifications appearing here for the first time present a somewhat more rounded portrait of a lion in winter than the original article, which (as always seems the case) suffered somewhat from space limitations.

AFTER RETIRING FROM THE Notre Dame presidency in 1987, Father Hesburgh was fond of sharing—and living—a personal credo, mentioned in the previous chapter, for facing one's later years: "Do as much as you can, as well as you can, as long as you can, and don't complain about the things you can no longer do."

Wisely commonsensical, plain-spoken, and direct, Father Hesburgh's refrain, frequently repeated in interviews and speeches, defined a post-presidential afterlife as eventful, in its way, as his earlier years. Abiding continuities—priestly service, devotion to Notre Dame, working for international peace and justice, and strengthening American higher education—occupied his days and created a crowded calendar. On occasion he was amusingly self-disparaging about his advancing age, but his schedule would have tired someone half his years.

Special Masses, formal meetings, arranged talks, office appointments, off-campus trips, and an endless succession of media interviews and dinners competed for his time and challenged any concept of conventional rest-on-your-oars retirement. Honors and awards also came with such frequency that during much of his twilight he remained quite visible, never far from the limelight. Though he had always been referred to as Father, age brought new self-realization. "I enjoy the role of being everybody's grandfather," he once told me, and it was a line he liked to repeat. That he viewed Dwight Eisenhower, a favorite president, in a similar way added to the meaning of the self-description.

When Father Hesburgh left the president's office in the Main Building, he wanted his successor, Rev. Edward A. Malloy, C.S.C., to have a clear field to develop his own administration. After hearing jibes for all the traveling he'd done the preceding thirty-five years, the priest still thought it best to take to the road—for pleasure this time—and remain absent from Notre Dame for a full year.

Accompanied by Rev. Edmund P. Joyce, C.S.C., his executive vice president throughout his term and his closest friend, Father Hesburgh set off in a motor home to explore the western United States, later taking to the air and sea to visit places around the world. They did not abandon their spiritual duties along the way; they even served several months as chaplains on the *Queen Elizabeth II* during a 1988 world cruise. No longer obliged to get somewhere for a scheduled event or meeting, they could wander as tourists, enjoying the sites without university worries and responsibilities. In getting away they created breathing room for the new administration and assumed a different pace. As Father Hesburgh later said, "Retirement had begun with a bang, not a whimper."

Father Hesburgh recounted the adventures (and occasional misadventures) of the months removed from Notre Dame in his diary-based narrative, *Travels with Ted & Ned*, published by Doubleday in 1992. Two years earlier Doubleday had released his autobiography, *God, Country, Notre Dame*, a critically admired bestseller that in hardcover and paperback editions circulated more than five hundred thousand copies. And, in 1994, he assembled, edited, and introduced *The Challenge and Promise of a Catholic University*, a wide-ranging series of essays for the Notre Dame Press.

That book projects took up so much of his early retirement seemed only natural. By then Father Hesburgh worked in the book-lined office on the thirteenth floor of the library that since 1987 bore his name and to which he had given his prized collection of author-inscribed volumes. The original benefaction in 1993 of 1,200 autographed copies (from world notables in politics, science, religion, business, and the arts) grew to nearly 2,000 titles during subsequent years. A lifelong lover of books was leaving behind for others those with special meaning for him.

Notwithstanding his publishing productivity (three volumes between 1990 and 1994) and occasional op-ed columns for the *Wall Street Journal*, *Washington Post*, and other publications through the first decade of the twenty-first century, Father Hesburgh never cut himself off from the life of the university and the outer world for solitary, bookish pursuits. As had happened throughout his presidency, invitations to serve on boards and commissions or to conduct special projects arrived with regularity.

For example, in 1989 he was named cochair of the Knight Commission on Intercollegiate Athletics, work that encompassed the better part of a decade. A year later he was elected to a six-year term on the Harvard University Board of Overseers. The first priest on Harvard's board, he subsequently was chosen president of the overseers in both 1994 and 1995. In 1991 President George H. W. Bush nominated Father Hesburgh to serve on the board of directors of the U. S. Institute of Peace, a post he held until 1999. Other, less time-consuming appointments came along, and he fitted them into his busy, certainly unretiring schedule.

Within Notre Dame, three programs he was instrumental in launching—the Kroc Institute for International Peace Studies, the Kellogg Institute for International Studies, and the Center for Civil and Human Rights—continued to receive his special attention. Father Hesburgh made a point of participating in their meetings, conferences and other activities, not only to show his support but also to stay up to date in the thinking and policy initiatives related to areas he considered critically important.

In fact, a unifying lesson of the priest's post-presidency came to be the enduring value of sustained, self-directed continuing education. His constant openness to new knowledge helped him develop a more rounded and deeper understanding of America and the world. "You learn a great deal because you've got to get down to primary sources," he told me, noting the study time required when he had served on the National Science Board, the Commission on Civil Rights, the International Atomic Energy Agency, and later the Knight Commission and the U.S. Institute of Peace.

With many outside appointments, Father Hesburgh began with limited knowledge of the complexities of certain subjects. Describing his preparation in one interview, he said, "I read what seemed like a million pages and spent days on end in hearings. So if you've got curiosity and if you read widely, you can take on almost any tough job—pick it up, get on top of it, and be able to go in and talk in the Senate and the House, hold press conferences and even argue with the president—but you've got to really work hard at it."

Quick to master complex data and multivolume reports, Father Hesburgh always probed the moral dimension of a subject. Ethical and spiritual concerns were never very far from the scientific, social, or academic matters that engaged him. In his view, moral inquiry deserved deliberation in conjunction with substantive considerations.

Looking back in 2005 during an extended interview about his retirement years, he talked first about his appointment on the board of the U.S. Institute of Peace. Mentioning trips to Kosovo, the Middle East, and elsewhere, he said, "Every time there was a crisis we got into it." Father Hesburgh brought to his work with the institute his own, distinct perspective. "Peace tends to be a bit nebulous," he explained, "but when you're applying it to practical political situations, it becomes a lot more concrete."

After taking another long puff on his cigar, he continued, "I think the methods of peace are multitudinous, but I like mediation where you can sit down with the two aggrieved parties and somehow work it out between them. It reminds me a great deal of what I've done as a priest in trying to fix up marriages that are going sour. You've got to understand both sides, and you have to be fair with both sides—but you need to be firm about what steps are needed to achieve peace in a family or a nation or in the world."

His own efforts as priest-peacemaker help to explain why he devoted so much of himself to seeing peace studies flourish at Notre Dame. Pointing out that "we are the largest endowed peace endeavor in the whole world," he enjoyed telling how the Kroc Institute for International Peace Studies came into being in 1986 and ultimately received nearly $70 million from Joan Kroc.

"It all started with a talk I didn't want to give in San Diego, because I was on the alumni circuit, giving talks every night," he recalled. Joan Kroc, widow of McDonald's founder Ray Kroc, happened to be in the audience and became interested in supporting scholarly work focusing on conflict resolution. Initial gifts during his final years as president continued after he left office, with Mrs. Kroc leaving the institute $50 million when she died in 2003.

Although Father Hesburgh called his service on the Harvard overseers "a wonderful experience" because it provided him "an inside track on everything going on at Harvard," he found cochairing the Knight Commission demanding and, at times, depressing. Investigations by the commission revealed the dark underside of amateur sports on campuses across America. In the priest's pull-no-punches parlance, "We developed a picture of intercollegiate athletics that would make you want to vomit. It was out of control and getting worse."

Formed two years after he retired, the commission singled out the seeking and spending of money as the overriding problem. Ticket sales for games and postseason contests—along with lucrative television contracts—contributed to rule-challenging searches for athletes, the so-called talent, in the revenue-producing sports of football and basketball. Some of the prized recruits cared little about receiving an education, a situation more than a few schools were willing to abet by looking the other way or designing less than rigorous curricula, such as awarding academic credit for watching game films of a team's next opponent. "We turned up one guy who couldn't read or write," Father Hesburgh remembered, "and he was in a university."

In particular, according to the civil rights–minded cleric, minority athletes were vulnerable to exploitation: "They were simply used for four years and then thrown out on the garbage heap, not having any degree or any skill because they were fed kindergarten courses during what was supposed to be a university experience. They were not educated at all. They were just used."

Father Hesburgh approached his work on the Knight Commission as he had so many earlier assignments: with moral concern merged with a sense of injustice that cried out for change. In a widely quoted statement from the commission's early deliberations, he put the matter bluntly: "If some schools don't want to join this reform effort, they can form their own outlaw league for illiterate players."

By the time Father Hesburgh concluded his service on the Knight Commission, the NCAA, which governs intercollegiate athletics, had formally adopted about 90 percent of the commission's proposals for correction and improvement. He wasn't completely satisfied, though, because he had pushed for a particular change that hadn't been implemented. "I always held for one academic remedy," he recalled. "My remedy was that if you didn't graduate at least half of your athletes in football and basketball, you would be disqualified from winning the championship in your conference or playing in postseason games. That one move, I thought, would really take care of the problem in a hurry."

Trying to reform collegiate sports provoked criticism of the Knight Commission, often directed personally at Father Hesburgh. "The super jocks thought we were out of our minds," he told me years later. But being on the receiving end of disapproval was nothing new for someone who'd spent much of his lifetime trying to solve thorny problems in the klieg-light glare of media scrutiny.

During his retirement years, one particular activity prompted bitter opposition, especially among the more politically partisan Notre Dame alumni. In 1994 Father Hesburgh was named cochair of what was called a Presidential Legal Expense Trust established to raise money for the personal legal expenses of Bill and Hillary Clinton related to pre–White House business and conduct. At the time, the Clintons were under investigation for a failed real-estate investment in Arkansas, known as Whitewater, and the president was defending himself against a sexual harassment lawsuit by a former Arkansas state employee, Paula Corbin Jones.

The other cochair of the trust was former U.S. Attorney General Nicholas Katzenbach, and trustees included John Brademas, longtime member of the House of Representatives from Indiana and president emeritus of New York University; Michael Sovern, Columbia University's president emeritus; and Elliot Richardson, a cabinet member in several Republican administrations.

Despite the distinguished participants and the strict restrictions on gifts (a maximum of $1,000 per year "only from individual citizens other than federal government employees, not from corporations, labor unions, partnerships, political action committees or other entities"), the trust was called—in the headline of one *New York Times* editorial—"The Tainted Defense Fund," and a federal suit filed in Washington's U.S. District Court sought to shut it down. More controversial than successful, the trust ended its work after three and a half years, with the Clintons still owing more than $3 million in legal expenses. In its last year, 1997, legal and administrative costs to keep the trust operating exceeded the donations it received.

Throughout the experience Father Hesburgh considered the higher purpose of his involvement, frequently commenting, "I agreed to do this for the presidency, not necessarily for this president. I would have done it for any president." In his view, it seemed "unfair for a sitting president" to worry about enormous legal fees "while he had more important national and international concerns to face." Speaking candidly to me, he commented, "It just struck me the guy was up a creek . . . with people suing him and one thing or another."

In retrospect, almost a decade after the trust ended, Hesburgh summed up the endeavor within a larger context. "I would say the whole thing was one of the most unproductive things I was ever involved in," he said. "Holding out a hand to a guy when he's down didn't seem to me to be a terrible thing to do, although those things tend to break down Democratic and Republican. Republicans hate you, and Democrats love you. But I was always nonpolitical. I never endorsed anybody. There was some criticism, but I just took it as a tempest in a teapot. I don't have any terribly bad memory about it."

Although Father Hesburgh saw his involvement in institutional terms—helping the presidency—Bill Clinton, as a person, impressed him, particularly at their first meeting on June 24, 1993. Father Hesburgh was in Washington on business for the U.S. Institute of Peace when he received a call summoning him immediately to the White House. Ushered into the Oval Office, he recalled being asked, "Is it true that you were ordained a priest fifty years ago today?" He confirmed the fact, and Clinton said, "Then I think it is proper you should be in this house and in this office so I can congratulate you on what you have done for your Church as well as what you have done for your country."

Seven years later, on July 13, 2000, Father Hesburgh told this story in the rotunda of the U.S. Capitol, with the president and leaders of the House and Senate present, as he received the Congressional Gold Medal, the first ever conferred on someone in advanced education. The Gold Medal is the highest award Congress can bestow, and its recipients include George Washington, Winston Churchill, Mother Teresa, and Nelson Mandela.

In his remarks, Clinton, who interrupted Middle East peace talks at Camp David to present the medal, turned to Hesburgh and said, "I would say that the most important thing about you and the greatest honor you will ever wear around your neck is the collar you have worn for fifty-seven years."

Later in the proceedings, Father Hesburgh echoed the president's words. "You might say this is the happiest day of my life, but it really isn't. The happiest day of my life was when I was ordained a Catholic priest, lying stretched out on my face in the sanctuary of Sacred Heart Church at Notre Dame. I was filled with the Holy Spirit, who has fortunately stayed with me all these fifty-seven years. I was filled with a conviction that I wasn't being ordained for myself, that I was an instrument in the hands of God. I wasn't to think that I simply belonged to Catholics; I belonged to every human being."

As priestly instrument and shepherd to all, Father Hesburgh earned widespread recognition during the years he served as Notre Dame's president—most notably in 1964, when President Lyndon Johnson awarded him the Medal of Freedom, the nation's highest civilian honor—and subsequently throughout his retirement years. In 1998, for instance, Indiana Governor Frank O'Bannon named him one of five Hoosier Millennium Treasures. In 2004 the NCAA bestowed on him the inaugural Gerald Ford Award for his decades of leadership in intercollegiate athletics, and the following year the College Sports Information Directors of America gave him the Dick Enberg Award for his commitment to the values of education and academics within collegiate sports. In 2006 Indiana's highest tribute, the Sachem Award, was bestowed on him, and, in 2010 Catholic Charities USA announced that Father Hesburgh was the recipient of a specially commissioned Centennial Medal for his efforts to reduce poverty.

Special honors arrived for him so constantly that the reception area and sitting room of his office in the Hesburgh Library took on an award motif, with etched vases and bowls sitting chockablock with engraved sculptures and medallions. They competed for a visitor's attention with pictures of the priest with presidents, popes, and other immediately recognizable figures.

Most remarkably, at the time of his death he had received 150 honorary degrees, the most ever awarded to one person. Though pleased with the far-flung, colleague-sanctioned acclaim within higher education, Father Hesburgh tried to keep his feat in perspective. Each certificate and doctoral hood was given to the Notre Dame Archives. "After I kick off," he told a reporter in 2002, "they might display them someplace. But that's only because I wouldn't be around to stop them."

Honors were also named for him. The Association of Catholic Colleges and Universities created the Rev. Theodore M. Hesburgh, CSC, Award for outstanding contributions to Catholic education. TIAA-CREF (the retirement and investment firm established for educators) instituted the Theodore M. Hesburgh Award for Leadership Excellence to recognize distinction in faculty development that enhances undergraduate teaching.

Although recognitions tended to look back on prior achievements, Father Hesburgh in retirement focused on the present and the future. A month shy of turning eighty-eight in 2005, he told me, "I have a full schedule every day and very little time off. I'd rather have it that way, but now it's concentrated and it's local and it's all Notre Dame one way or another." Remarkably, this pattern continued until a month or so before his death.

In 2007 he participated in a ninetieth birthday celebration in Washington that featured a visit to the White House and a ceremony at the Smithsonian Institution. At the event, attended by government leaders and other public figures, a photograph of him hand in hand and shoulder to shoulder with civil rights leader Martin Luther King Jr. was unveiled and added to the permanent collection of the National Portrait Gallery. A copy also hung in the White House during the presidency of Barack Obama.

On St. Patrick's Day in 2012, Father Hesburgh became an Irish citizen in a ceremony that brought Enda Kenny, the taoiseach (or prime minister) of Ireland, to Notre Dame. In receiving his new Irish passport, Father Hesburgh talked about using it for another transatlantic trip to visit the birthplace of his grandfather Martin Murphy, who immigrated to America in 1857. A year later, the chief of navy chaplains formally named the priest an honorary U.S. Navy chaplain, fulfilling in a poignant way an early dream. After his ordination, he often said how much he wanted to be a navy chaplain during World War II, but assignments at Notre Dame prevented him from doing so.

An intrepid traveler for over eight decades—in 1993 he remarked "I've been in 160 countries and around the world many times"—Father Hesburgh reached the point where his failing eyesight prevented him from reading an airplane ticket or the room number at a hotel. The last major appointment he accepted was one made by President George W. Bush in 2001 to serve on the Commission on Presidential Scholars. It was the sixteenth time a president had called on the priest to serve his nation in one capacity or another.

Shortly thereafter, his condition of near-blindness forced him to conclude all service on boards and commissions. "When I came to that point," he admitted to me, "I decided I'm getting off everything." In rare instances, he would make a trip off-campus, but private transportation and someone to serve as a guide became necessary.

Father Hesburgh's final visit to the nation's capital was timed to coincide with his ninety-sixth birthday in 2013, and he had several friends from Notre Dame to assist and make the trip highly rewarding. He met with President Obama in the White House and then went to the U.S. Capitol for a tribute in the Rayburn Room.

This celebration of Father Hesburgh's life and achievements was co-hosted by Speaker John Boehner and House Minority Leader Nancy Pelosi. In his remarks, Vice President Joe Biden spoke directly to the guest of honor, saying, "You're one of the most powerful unelected officials this nation has ever seen."

For an avid reader and constant writer, macular degeneration can be a cruel sentence to years of darkness. Father Hesburgh, however, adapted to the challenge, brushing it off as the "nonsense that happens" in a long life. In place of reading, he listened to audiobooks provided by the Library of Congress— as many as thirty a month. To help him keep up with current affairs, students stopped by his office to read the *New York Times* and other publications to him.

"Once your eyes go, you can't drive, you can't read, you can't write," he said. "I can't even write a few notes down for a talk. Everything has to come out of your head and your memory." To emphasize the challenge of speaking without a prompting sheet of any kind, he remarked to me, "When I get up to give a sermon, I can't have anything in front of me."

Father Hesburgh recalled the sense of trepidation he felt prior to delivering the eulogy for Father Joyce before a crowded Basilica of the Sacred Heart on May 5, 2004. "I remember when Father Ned died, I just thought about it for two days. There were a million thoughts, of course, because we'd been together so long. Climbing up the steps of the pulpit, I said, 'Lord, I don't know what I'm going to say, but I hope you'll keep me down below fifteen minutes.' I just started out, and the Holy Spirit is a fine inspiration on all these things. My first prayer in the morning and the last one at night is 'Come, Holy Spirit.'"

For listeners in the congregation and readers of the published version, the elegiac and moving remarks were among the most memorable he ever uttered. A colleague, confidant, and friend was movingly brought to life—and thanked—at the funeral Mass. Near the end, Father Hesburgh said, "I know we're going to miss you, Ned, but we all go when the time comes and your time has come. I guess the best I can say is thanks, Ned, for those long days of caring, those long nights of work in the cause of Our Lady's school, to make it better and more worthy of her.

"Thanks for all those prayers we needed, when we needed them very much. Thanks for all the wisdom that kept me from making a lot of silly mistakes at times. And thanks just for being a brother to your brothers [in Holy Cross], being a friend to all of us, being a willing and dedicated priest, ready to act like a priest when I needed it, and God knows I needed it a good deal.

"I guess all we can say is, Ned, we'll be seeing you. I truly believe that. There will be more days when we can get around and talk about the glories of this wonderful place and all the wonderful people. There will be days ahead when we can look back and thank God we got through without too many scrapes and bruises. But especially, I think, we'll look back with great gratitude for that wonderful grace Jesus gave us both in making us priests."

Father Hesburgh's inability to read and write necessitated changes in how he communicated, but he was willing to try other means and modern media to convey his thoughts to a large audience. In 2004 the Notre Dame Alumni Association produced a documentary, *A Man for All Generations: Life's Lessons from Fr. Ted Hesburgh, C.S.C.*, while a year later Family Theater Productions came out with *God, Country, Notre Dame: The Story of Father Ted Hesburgh, C.S.C.*

Both productions featured the still-telegenic cleric reflecting on subjects he felt deeply about and on his own experiences. Always articulate, often eloquent, he talked without notes or much preparation about the virtues of a well-lived life, the importance of prayer, and the need to face death with courage. Inspirational homilies of hope, vivid phrasing, and his reassuring voice made for compelling television.

In the Alumni Association production, Father Hesburgh was the sole speaker; in the other, several friends and admirers (including three former presidents: Gerald Ford, Jimmy Carter, and George H. W. Bush) offered statements about Father Hesburgh and his public service to supplement the priest's reminiscences and recollections.

In 2001, the year of his last presidential appointment, Father Hesburgh also published one of his last major statements in *The Chronicle of Higher Education*. Shaped from a speech he delivered at Notre Dame, the essay was, in its way, a lament that asked a pointed question: "Where Are College Presidents' Voices on Important Public Issues?"

Contrasting the way he and earlier academic leaders took stands on controversial issues with the relative silence of current presidents, Father Hesburgh wondered aloud and then in print, "Where we once had a fellowship of public intellectuals, do we now have insulated chief executives intent on keeping the complicated machinery of American higher education running smoothly?"

Characteristically, Father Hesburgh evaluated the hesitancy to speak out in terms of its more encompassing consequence. He recalled the "contentious times" of the 1960s and 1970s, with their turmoil on campuses and across the nation at large: "Painful as those days were, however, they taught a powerful lesson: We cannot urge students to have the courage to speak out unless we are willing to do so ourselves. The true antidote to the public's view that colleges are simply ivory towers of intellectual dilettantism is engagement with important public issues—however difficult and thorny those issues may be."

Father Hesburgh's concern for and interest in students never dimmed during his retirement years. Indeed, when he started to decline off-campus assignments, his schedule opened up and allowed for even more student interaction. Talking in his office, he spoke in a tone of contentment and satisfaction: "Any student is welcome here, and there's hardly a day goes by that I don't have two or three students. They all have different problems, and they have opportunities, and occasionally they say they haven't been to confession in a long time. I say, 'We can take care of that in three minutes,' which we do."

Besides the constant round of office meetings, Father Hesburgh also offered Mass in dormitory chapels whenever asked and frequently said the rosary with student groups. His macular degeneration seriously reduced his ability to focus on faces, but students recognized Father Ted, approaching him at the library or as he made his way around campus to various activities. He never avoided a chance to talk with an individual student or a group. Invariably, he asked specific questions about what was happening in Notre Dame classrooms and in their lives.

In an irony of his retirement, the priest-academic who began his career at Notre Dame in 1945 as a faculty member in the Department of Religion engaged in more teaching during his retirement years than he'd ever been able to do as president. "I teach a lot of classes," he said with a smile of satisfaction. "I tell students the things I can talk about: the university and its history, science, atomic energy, civil rights, world development, peace issues and so forth," he explained to me. "They always have something pertinent that I can address. I probably have taught more classes than some faculty here in the sense that I have this kind of thing happening all the time, probably at least forty times in a semester. It's always a different group, and it's always fun."

Father Hesburgh's open-door policy extended beyond students to faculty, staff, alumni, and campus visitors. "Everything I do now is for Notre Dame, and I give it a full run every day," he said during our conversation in 2005. "I'm a nut on correspondence, so every letter that arrives every day is answered before I leave in the afternoon."

The Notre Dame Archives is the repository of Father Hesburgh's papers as well as the honorary degrees and other memorabilia. Each year of his retirement generated an average of three or four filing cabinet drawers of letters, papers, and official reports.

In the autumn of 2004, Father Hesburgh fell in his residence at Corby Hall, opening a cut in his head that required medical attention and stitches. Talking with others, he decided it was time to move to Holy Cross House, an assisted living and health care facility for retired priests next to Moreau Seminary on the Notre Dame campus.

After fifty-three years of residence, leaving Corby Hall—adjacent to Sacred Heart and close by the Main Building—wasn't easy. Yet Hesburgh's attitude was both realistic and future-oriented: you do what you have to do. He quickly entered into the rhythm of Holy Cross House, with its late morning Mass for the community and its daily meals for socializing. Many days, however, lunches or dinners at the Morris Inn or elsewhere on campus as well as in South Bend interrupted the routine.

During the academic year, with full afternoons devoted to work in his office and several evenings each week filled with student or university engagements, he looked forward to taking breaks during summers at Land O' Lakes, Notre Dame's 7,500-acre, thirty-lake environmental research center located on both sides of the state line between Wisconsin and the Upper Peninsula of Michigan. For decades, Father Hesburgh spent a few weeks each summer there, engaging in the only hobby he loved: fishing.

"It has therapeutic effects," he said to me, warming to a subject he clearly loved to discuss. "I'm out in a boat in the middle of a lake, and it's quiet and peaceful. No telephones. No letters. The sun is generally shining, and I'm getting sunburned, but I'm also catching fish, which is fun. You've got to have something for fun."

Though his vision problems made fishing much more difficult, he was still able to enjoy his favorite recreational pastime. "I can see enough to see the shore and to see the trees on the shore, and I don't throw into the trees. I throw into the shore. I can see enough to fish decently if I'm casting to shore from a boat. If it were trout fishing, it would be a lot more difficult."

One of Father Hesburgh's favorite fishing yarns about Land O' Lakes involved the time in 1959 when the entire Commission on Civil Rights flew there to debate and draft a report for the president and Congress. Despite ideological and regional differences, the six members were remarkably like-minded in their conclusions and proposals.

As the priest tells the story in *God, Country, Notre Dame*, "When we met with President Eisenhower in September, he said he could not understand how a commission with three Democrats who were all Southerners, and two Republicans and an independent who were all Northerners, could possibly vote six-to-zero on eleven recommendations and five-to-one on the other. I told Ike that he had not appointed just

Republicans and Democrats or Northerners and Southerners, he had appointed six fishermen. I told him about Land O' Lakes and he commented, 'We've got to put more fishermen on commissions and have more reports written at Land O' Lakes, Wisconsin.'"

During a lifetime of posing for pictures, either alone or with some luminary, Father Hesburgh preferred one shot in particular. It caught him sitting in a boat, holding a rod, and sporting a full beard. Looking enough like Ernest Hemingway's younger brother to draw double-take comparisons, the photo is featured on the cover of the hardcover and paperback editions of *Travels with Ted & Ned*. A framed print was also prominently displayed in his library office.

In the classic essay "Self-Reliance," nineteenth-century American philosopher and poet Ralph Waldo Emerson wrote, "An institution is the lengthened shadow of one man." Father Hesburgh's commitment to Notre Dame reflected the acuity of that insight, with today's campus offering visible portions of that lengthened shadow: the Hesburgh Library, the Hesburgh Center for International Studies, the Hesburgh Program in Public Service, the Hesburgh Lecture Series of the Alumni Association, and so on.

Several endowed chairs bear his name, and in 2006 Notre Dame established the Keough-Hesburgh Professorships to attract to campus noted scholar-teachers to advance the university's Catholic mission and character. A gift of former chairman of the Board of Trustees Donald R. Keough and his family, Keough-Hesburgh Professorships currently exist in several academic departments across the university.

In 2009 Mark and Stacey Yusko created the Hesburgh-Yusko Scholars Program to foster the education and development of future leaders inspired by Father Hesburgh's vision and commitment. Each Hesburgh-Yusko Scholar—there were twenty-five in the first class, a number that remained constant as an objective—received a $25,000 merit scholarship annually throughout four undergraduate years, as well as funding for four summer enrichment experiences. The program, with its emphasis on educating future leaders, helped put Father Hesburgh's own vision into action.

Selecting the most satisfying university legacy wasn't easy for Hesburgh, but, pressed to choose, he named the library: "I walk through here, and I see thousands of students and millions of books. When we built this place, we had two hundred and fifty thousand books. Now we've passed three million, plus two and a half million more on microfiche. That's a lot of books."

As he continued to talk, Father Hesburgh kept puffing on his cigar. Asked whether his smoky habit of long standing created any problem at a place with a no-smoking policy in every building, he said, "This is the only room in the library where I can smoke. If someone would say to me, 'How come you're the only one smoking in here?' I'd say, 'After all, I got my name on it. After all, I got the money to build the place. After all, I built up these book collections. If I can't smoke here, I'll work somewhere else, where I can.'"

Still, he once told the magazine *Cigar Aficionado*, "I don't want life to be defined by a cigar" and "Life is full of checks and balances, and it's important not to go overboard on anything—except God, if you will." Having offered this high-toned hedging for publication, Father Hesburgh was willing to go just so far in adapting to the rules on campus after he left the presidency. An aside about Notre Dame's almost universal smoke-free environment suggested an individual's frustration, largely because it posed a problem involving his well-established and decades-old routine for work and conversations at the university.

For Father Hesburgh, however, the Deity was the center of his life—the first word in the title of his autobiography and the only reason "to go overboard." A priest's priest, he constantly emphasized the power and necessity of prayer throughout his retirement years. Asserting that "one of the greatest things is just to get up every day and serve God as best you can," Hesburgh didn't hesitate to confront his own mortality: "I pray that when the time comes I can be as courageous about facing death as I was about facing life."

This prayer also carried with it a personal request, one he made during the Mass celebrating the fiftieth anniversary of his ordination in 1993 and repeated, privately and publicly, in his later years. The "one last grace" he wanted above all others was the chance "to offer the Holy Sacrifice of the Mass every day of my life until I die. Then I'll die happy."

His prayer was answered. On the morning of February 26, 2015, a couple months before his ninety-eighth birthday, Father Hesburgh offered Mass in the morning. Twelve hours later he passed away, shortly after completing another religious ritual of his long and crowded life.

He and a nurse's aide at Holy Cross House, Amivi Gbologan, who assisted him throughout his last year, recited the rosary together. Originally from the small African country of Togo, a former colony of France, the aide only knew how to say the rosary in French. That, though, didn't pose a problem for the multilingual priest.

Someone with rudimentary knowledge of Notre Dame history might point out the special appropriateness of this other "last grace" near the hour of his death. Notre Dame's founder, Rev. Edward Sorin, C.S.C., was born and grew up in

France, and Father Hesburgh's final prayers were in the native language of his most significant predecessor. Though a century separated them, both Holy Cross priests were dreamers and builders with lengthened shadows—and golden, as well as enduring, legacies.

Melanie Chapleau served as Father Hesburgh's all-purpose and always proficient assistant after he retired from the Notre Dame presidency. No task was too large—or too small—for her to do. Photo courtesy of Matt Cashore.

Epilogue

For over a quarter century, Melanie Chapleau served as Officer Assistant to Rev. Theodore M. Hesburgh, C.S.C. The title, though lofty and impressive, never did justice to her responsibilities as schedule keeper, word processor, file curator, correspondence reader, and so forth. This world-class gatekeeper and aide-de-camp's birthday is December 5. On that day in 2014, Rev. Austin Collins, C.S.C., a professor of sculpture at Notre Dame and a noted sculptor outside the classroom, decided to put together a small surprise party for Melanie in Father Hesburgh's office suite. (Father Collins and Rev. Paul Doyle, C.S.C., rector of Dillon Hall, with unfailing generosity, helped Father Hesburgh in his later years to attend campus functions and to make short trips. In addition, both priests often looked in on the oldest member of the Holy Cross order to see how he was doing.)

Melanie arrived back from lunch to find a dozen or so friends duly assembled in the large meeting room near her work area to wish her well. With several of the invited needing to return to work, the group sang "Happy Birthday" and started to pass around pieces of the celebratory cake. Then, a few minutes later than he usually arrived at his office each afternoon, Father Hesburgh joined the revelry.

In a trice Father Hesburgh took command from his wheelchair, asking everyone assembled to sing "Happy Birthday" once more. When we reached the last familiar word, the priest made a request: "If I might have the floor for a moment." He proceeded to praise Melanie and other women at Notre Dame who worked diligently for the people in leadership roles at the university. He also singled out Helen Hosinski, his right-hand woman during his presidency and before. Like Melanie, Helen kept everything straight for a man of many commitments and demands—and she did it for almost a half century.

It was a warm, sincere, eloquent tribute. From decades of honoring those with whom he worked at Notre Dame, in government posts, and elsewhere, he knew precisely what to say for such an occasion. This time, however, there was a touching, bittersweet postscript.

Not long following his brief remarks, Father Hesburgh again called on the group to sing "Happy Birthday." Afterwards he raised his voice, "If I might have the floor for a moment." What we heard, almost word for word, was a replay of his recently delivered encomium for Melanie and other women assisting administrators at the university.

Someone without any expertise in psychology or geriatrics should have enough sense to avoid speculating or trying to diagnose what happened. But the interplay, in some cases rivalry, between short-term and long-term memory seemed on display that afternoon. Father Hesburgh was concentrating so intently on recognizing Melanie—on leading the singing and then offering the appropriate verbal coda for the little celebration—that he repeated himself. He wanted to make sure that he spoke his piece, as people would have said when he was a young man. That in itself was uppermost in his ninety-seven-and-a-half-year-old mind.

A couple weeks later I headed to France to begin research for a magazine article. Upon returning in January, I needed to get ready for the launch of the new semester and never made time to stop by Father Hesburgh's office or his apartment at Holy Cross House. In mid-February, e-mails began to arrive, reporting rapid weight loss since Christmas and a general decline. It was a cold, bleak time.

On a Thursday night, February 26, 2015, Father Hesburgh passed away. Interestingly, even fittingly, the first public celebration of the Mass in the colonies of the New World had taken place in Philadelphia 283 years earlier, on February 26, 1732. The figure many journalists referred to as "the American Pope" in the 1960s and 1970s had himself offered Mass earlier in the day.

For well over a decade, university committees had worked to organize the events for saying farewell. At the wake in Sacred Heart Basilica the night before the funeral, Rev. Edward A. Malloy, C.S.C., who succeeded Father Hesburgh as Notre Dame's president, provided a pitch-perfect homily, and the next day Rev. John I. Jenkins, C.S.C., the current president, delivered a salutary eulogy at the funeral. That evening former president Jimmy Carter, Cardinal Theodore McCarrick, alumna and former secretary of state Condoleezza Rice, and former football coach Lou Holtz were among the notable representatives from different realms who remembered Father Hesburgh, the man and his work, at a special tribute, attended by thousands, in the Joyce Athletic and Convocation Center.

Former Wyoming Senator Alan Simpson, who had served with Father Hesburgh on the Select Committee on Immigration and Refugee Policy, evoked both laughter and applause when he recited the earthy "common credo" that the priest and his politician-friend shared: "'If you're damned if you do and damned if you don't, then do.' Don't ever forget that one, young people." Former president Carter repeated a judgment he first articulated in 1977, when he received an honorary degree from Notre Dame: "Father Ted Hesburgh has been the most consistent and effective spokesman for the rights of human beings that I have ever known."

Not surprisingly, from my perspective, Notre Dame undergraduates, the "young people" Simpson acknowledged, provided the most moving moments of the public's opportunity to pay their collective respects. Residents of campus dormitories slowly filed by the casket throughout the night after the wake. Following the funeral, each inch of space from Sacred Heart to the Holy Cross Cemetery, a distance of a half mile, was occupied on both sides of the road by students (some places along the route three or four deep) and a sprinkling of alumni or South Bend residents. Shivering from the teeth-chattering cold, many of the young men and women dressed up for the occasion, with some fellows wearing formal attire for the occasion.

Undergrads in 2015 weren't even born when Father Hesburgh retired as president in 1987. (The majority came into the world in 1994 or later.) Yet they felt what he had accomplished earlier had touched their own lives. Some had stopped by his office for a visit and a blessing. Some were in classes or scholarship programs that involved him as a guest speaker. Most were beneficiaries of his efforts to strengthen academic departments or to develop new ones, to enhance spiritual life on campus, to lead the university in welcoming women as undergraduates, or to raise the resources needed for building additional research and teaching facilities. Then there was his work as a conscientious citizen of the United States and the world. He had done so much that enduring frigid temperatures wasn't that great of a sacrifice.

During the last couple decades of his life, Father Hesburgh was both priest and presence, a person of theology, pedagogy, and, yes, mythology. Always approachable yet still a figure to revere, he was simply "Father Ted." Young people helped him to stay connected to what was new and different on campus, and he kept reaching out to them.

A decade before Father Hesburgh's death, our son, Mike, then a student residing in O'Neill Hall, reported that a dorm friend of his was studying on the thirteenth floor of the Hesburgh Library when he felt a tap on his shoulder. It was the library's namesake, and he wanted someone to serve the Mass he was going to offer in the small chapel close to his office.

"How cool is that, Dad?" our exuberant alumnus-to-be asked in a question that sounded more like an editorial comment. How many times were similar such stories repeated in dorms over the years? His common touch, a tap on a student's shoulder, could mean as much as a lecture about what it was like to chair the U.S. Commission on Civil Rights or to serve as a member of the Holy See's United Nations delegation.

That uncommon common touch extended beyond the students he encountered as president or president emeritus. Many years ago, a longtime custodian at Notre Dame told me that at one point he handled assignments in the Main Building, including the cleaning and shining of the hallways. On the night he started using a new floor-buffing machine, Father Hesburgh approached him and inquired about the multi-brush apparatus. The university's president wanted to know how it worked and then asked if he could try it out. Narrating the story, this jack-of-all-janitorial-trades smiled the entire time. His audience of one surmised that the anecdote had been recited, with pleasure, countless times in the past.

When Father Hesburgh died, many of the most engaging portions of the obituaries in the news media came from his own quotations, which journalists had saved to use again. One of them went this way: "I never thought I was a priest just to give sermons, and work in church, and hear confessions and marry people, bury people and so forth. I felt, I'm part of a big life out there, and I have got to contribute to that, one way or the other. I hope for the good." Another: "My basic principle is that you don't make decisions because they are easy, you don't make them because they are cheap, you don't make them because they're popular; you make them because they're right."

One more (and a favorite): "Catholics have a thing called the rosary, which is a kind of repetition of the Our Father then ten Hail Marys and it's, in a way, almost like something Eastern religions call a mantra. But in a way, saying the rosary, very often, like last night, I didn't get through it. I mean I wake up in the middle of the night and sometimes there's the rosary there and I fell asleep. When I was a youngster my Irish mother used to say, just say the rosary every night and if you fall asleep, the angels will finish it for you. It's funny, but that's an Irish mother for you."

The obituaries also pointed out that Father Hesburgh was a figure of "firsts": the first priest to serve as a U.S. ambassador, the first priest on Harvard's board of overseers, the first priest on the board of directors of the Chase Manhattan Bank, the first priest on the board of trustees of the Rockefeller Foundation, the first person in education to receive the Congressional Gold Medal, and the first person to be awarded 150 honorary degrees, the greatest number ever.

In a commentary tribute for *National Catholic Reporter*, Nathan O. Hatch, the president of Wake Forest University and a former history professor and administrator at Notre Dame, identified a paramount reason why Father Hesburgh was so successful in his approach and execution, namely his combination of "strong conviction with grace and generosity to all." The priest accepted polarities and could see merit in diametric viewpoints: "Father Ted could not be put in a conservative or liberal box. He clung to virtues on both sides of many modern debates. He was a huge champion of ROTC at Notre Dame and, at the same time, he championed peace studies and convinced Joan Kroc to endow magnificently the Kroc Institute for International Peace Studies. He was friend of the Rockefeller brothers and of Martin Luther King Jr., confidant of Republican and Democratic presidents, champion of the Catholic character of a place like Notre Dame and of intellectual freedom and institutional independence. Like Pope Francis, Father Ted never questioned the core traditions of the church, yet he never seemed defensive or resistant to fresh ways of thinking."

History teaches that no person is irreplaceable, but it's difficult to imagine another person like Father Hesburgh with the talent to juggle so many significant "jobs" (his word) in such diverse areas at the same time. In whatever he did, he became a moral voice in confronting an issue or problem. That voice was clear, consistent, and commanding. It was, to paraphrase Corinthians, a certain trumpet. Yet he also made himself available to students, alumni, friends, and visitors as though apportioning his time was never a worry.

John Quincy Adams once said, "If your actions inspire others to dream more, learn more, do more, and become more, you are a leader." Nearly a year after Father Hesburgh died, Selena Ponio, a student in a journalism class I was teaching, submitted a story about the continuing inspiration a leader's life can have. She recounted that Joachim Castellano, who is in his late thirties, had been working at a well-compensated job in Tokyo, but applied for a position at Notre Dame after he learned more about everything Father Hesburgh had accomplished.

The still-insatiable inquisitiveness of an aging newshound prompted me to track down Castellano, an educational technologist at the Center for the Study of Languages and Cultures. As he warmed to telling of his nearly 6,500-mile move to northern Indiana, he reported that his father had immigrated to the United States from the Philippines in 1966, in part because *he* became inspired by Notre Dame from listening to the school's football games broadcast on the Armed Forces Radio Network in his native land.

"I was in a country [Japan] that I still do love, and I was working at a job that I liked, so there was really no reason for me to leave," Castellano explained as he talked about his decision. "But, one Sunday morning in February of 2015, I came across the *New York Times* article about Father Hesburgh's passing. I knew he was president for a long time, but I didn't realize that he was much more than just a university president. He was an incredible human being."

Once he'd read the lengthy newspaper obituary, Castellano viewed a series of videos about Father Hesburgh on the Notre Dame website, which in retrospect he considers the principal motivation for him to apply for a position at Notre Dame. "It was definitely radical," he admitted, "but I feel like there are few times in your life where you can take chances like this. I just thought, hey, Father Hesburgh was a man of principle, and what an honor it would be to contribute to his mission to make Notre Dame one of the best universities in the world. I like to say that I was sent by Father Ted.

"In part I took the chance, took the risk, because of Father Ted and his life and his story. But it was also the chance to contribute to the greater good, especially with respect to interacting with students and inspiring them to do great things. I'm not saying I also want to be an international humanitarian exactly like Father Ted, but I at least want to make a positive contribution to student learning and the local community in my own way. If I could even accomplish one-sixteenth of what Father Ted did, I'd be pretty proud of my career."

Even in death, his humane magnetism continued to draw people to the characteristics he personified and represented through his involvement in religious, educational, governmental, and humanitarian initiatives. Yet, for someone who spent so much of his life at center stage, he adapted to over a quarter century of retirement without engaging in second-guessing or complaining unduly about his failing eyesight. A priest first (and always), he answered the requests of others as a daily duty. Often in our conversations, he'd say he didn't call any shots or make any decisions at Notre Dame. He was emeritus and no longer had a final say on anything. This was true but also, in its way, modest. Some benefactors enjoyed hearing about the value to the university of a sizable gift from leaders of the present—and one from the past. In that respect, and in meeting visitors to campus who wanted a handshake or a blessing, Father Hesburgh's door was always open.

What started for me as a cub reporter's juvenile curiosity about a figure frequently in the news developed into a continuing fascination that resulted in lengthy interviews for writing projects of one kind or another. And, to be sure, there were all of the open-ended, cigar-stoked conversations along with the campus activities I invited him to attend before and after his retirement. Over the decades, youthful interest blossomed into an authorial avocation and a most amicable association. I've even saved some cigars that he gave me as mementos of our afternoon visits.

To have watched Father Hesburgh for a half century provides an up-close, human study of different realms of history at the end of the twentieth century and into the beginning of the twenty-first. To have known him well for more than half that time enriches the memories and the meaning of those years. After Father Hesburgh died, I received a note from a graduate of the late 1990s with this tribute: "I'm glad I had the chance to meet him, even once. I'm afraid we won't see the likes of him again, but I'm glad we had the genuine article in our midst for so long."

Without a doubt, Theodore Martin Hesburgh was the genuine article.

ROBERT SCHMUHL is the Walter H. Annenberg–
Edmund P. Joyce Chair in American Studies and Journalism
at the University of Notre Dame, where he has taught since
1980. He is the author and editor of numerous books,
including *In So Many More Words: Arguments and Adventures*,
expanded edition (University of Notre Dame Press, 2010).